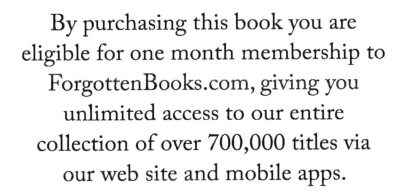

ISBN 978-0-331-08621-8
PIBN 10452224

Kleine Geschichten

für

Anfänger

SELECTED AND EDITED WITH NOTES AND COMPLETE
VOCABULARY

BY

ARNOLD WERNER-SPANHOOFD

DIRECTOR OF GERMAN INSTRUCTION IN THE HIGH SCHOOLS OF
WASHINGTON, D. C.

NEW YORK
D. APPLETON AND COMPANY
1904

PREFACE.

This little volume, as indicated by its title, aims to supply suitable reading matter for beginners in German. Care has been taken to introduce such selections only as are easy of construction, and without too great idiomatic and grammatical difficulties. The subject-matter is not beyond the capacity of first year students in either High School or Academy.

The selections are full of action, and thus can readily be made the basis for intelligent conversation in class. A few suggestive questions have been added to each selection, and other appropriate questions can easily be formed which will lead the student to a more thorough understanding and enjoyment of the story.

The notes have been made as helpful as possible, being complete in themselves, so that the little text may supplement any grammar, or may also be used independently. For the special benefit of beginners, the vocabulary has been so arranged that all strong and irregular forms which naturally would puzzle the student are introduced in their proper place in the alphabetical arrangement.

ARNOLD WERNER-SPANHOOFD.

WASHINGTON, D. C. 143902

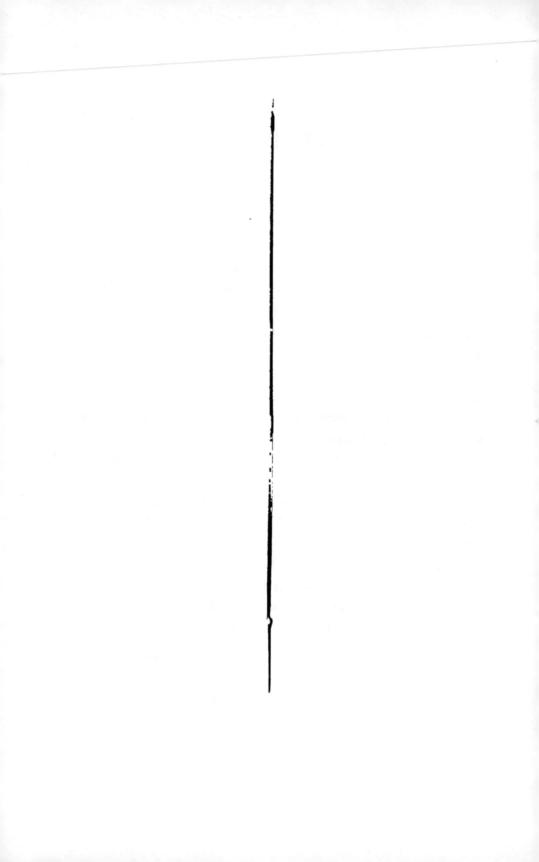

Kleine Geschichten für Anfänger.

1. Friedrich der Große.

Friedrich der Große[1] inspiziert[2] die Strafanstalt in Spandau[3] und erkundigt[4] sich bei jedem Gefangenen[5] nach seinem Verbrechen. Natürlich behaupten alle,[6] unschuldig zu sein.[7] Nur einer[8] unter ihnen ist aufrichtig und sagt zu dem König: „Ich bin ein großer Verbrecher und verdiene meine Strafe."

Da antwortet ihm[9] der König: „Was machst du[10] elender Kerl unter diesen braven[11] Leuten? Hinaus[12] mit dir!"

1. Was thut Friedrich der Große? — 2. Bei wem erkundigt er sich nach dem Verbrechen? — 3. Was behaupten alle Gefangenen? — 4. Ist kein Aufrichtiger unter den Gefangenen? — 5. Was sagt der aufrichtige Gefangene zu dem König? — 6. Was antwortet ihm der König?

2. Der Bettler.

Auf einer belebten Brücke steht täglich ein Bettler mit seinem Hunde. Der Hund trägt[1] um den Hals[2] eine Tafel mit der Inschrift: „Ich bin blind."

Ein mitleidiger, junger Mann wirft[3] dem Bettler

jeden Tag ein Geldſtück in den Hut.[2]   Eines Tages[4]
vergißt[5] er es, und der Bettler läuft ihm nach[6] und
ruft:

„Ach, geben Sie mir heute denn nichts, junger
Herr?“

„Was?“ ſagt der junge Mann erſtaunt, „ſind Sie
denn nicht blind?“

„Nein,“ antwortet der Bettler, „ich nicht,[7] ſondern
mein Hund.“

1. Wo ſteht der Bettler? — 2. Steht er dort allein? — 3. Was
trägt der Hund um den Hals? — 4. Welche Inſchrift hat die
Tafel? — 5. Wer geht jeden Tag über die Brücke? — 6. Was
thut der junge Mann? — 7. Was vergißt der junge Mann eines
Tages? — 8. Was ruft der Bettler? — 9. Wie iſt der junge
Mann, und was ſagt er zu dem Bettler? — 10. Iſt der Bettler
blind?

3. Kaiſer Barbaroſſa.[1]

Luſtige Muſikanten[2] beſchließen, dem alten Kaiſer
eine Nachtmuſik darzubringen.[3] In der Mitter=
nachtsſtunde[4] gehen[5] ſie im Mondenſchein den Berg
hinauf. Eben ſchlägt[6] unten im Dorfe die Glocke
zwölf. Beim zweiten Stück kommt die Prinzeſſin[7]
mit einem Lichte in der Hand[8] auf ſie zu[9] und winkt
ihnen zu folgen. Der Berg thut[10] ſich vor ihnen auf
und mit klingendem Spiele ziehen[11] ſie der Prinzeſſin
nach. Eſſen und Trinken[12] bekommen ſie reichlich,

aber niemand bietet[13] ihnen von den Schätzen an, die in großer Menge im Schlosse liegen.[14] Endlich, als der Morgen graut,[14] brechen[15] sie wieder auf. Der Kaiser nickt[16] ihnen freundlich zu, und die Prinzessin reicht jedem einen grünen Busch zum Andenken.[17] Als sie wieder aus dem Berge heraus[18] sind,[14] werfen[19] sie die Büsche fort und lachen und schelten über[20] solch ein[21] kaiserliches Geschenk; nur einer behält[22] den Busch und will ihn zum Andenken aufheben. Als er nach Hause[23] kommt, giebt[24] er seiner Frau den Busch und bemerkt in demselben Augenblicke, daß der Busch nicht mehr leicht ist, und daß alle Blätter und Zweige gediegenes Gold sind. Schnell laufen[25] die anderen auf den Berg zurück, um[26] ihre Büsche zu suchen; aber sie sind fort.

1. Was beschließen die lustigen Musikanten? — 2. Wann gehen sie den Berg hinauf? — 3. Was ist der Namen des Berges? — 4. Welche Stunde schlägt die Glocke im Dorfe? — 5. Was geschieht (geschehen) beim zweiten Stücke? — 6. Wohin folgen die Musikanten der Prinzessin? — 7. Was bietet man ihnen im Berge an? — 8. Wann brechen sie wieder auf? — 9. Was thun der Kaiser und die Prinzessin, als die Musikanten aufbrechen? — 10. Über was lachen und schelten die Musikanten? — 11. Warum wirft der eine Musikant seinen Busch nicht fort? — 12. Was bemerkt er, als er seiner Frau den Busch giebt? — 13. Was thun die anderen Musikanten, als sie dies hören? — 14. Finden sie ihre Büsche?

4. Der Hase und die Schnecke.

Eine Schnecke ging[1] mit einem Hasen ein Wett=
rennen ein. Als der Hase einige Sprünge gemacht
hatte, sah er, daß die Schnecke noch kaum von ihrem
Platze gekommen war.[2] Dann verspottete er ihre
thörichte Kühnheit[3] und sagte: „Plage dich nur[4] in
der heißen Mittagssonne; ich will indes unter dem
schattigen Busche ein Schläfchen halten."[5] Der Hase
legte sich und schlief[6] ein. Als er aber gegen[7] Sonnen=
untergang erwachte und eiligst zum Laufen[8] aufsprang,[9]
da saß die Schnecke schon am Ziele und rief[10] dem
kommenden Hasen, der vor Müdigkeit[11] keuchte, ent=
gegen: „Wer[12] langsam geht, kommt auch ans Ziel."[13]

1. Mit wem ging die Schnecke ein Wettrennen ein? — 2. Was
sah der Hase nach einigen Sprüngen? — 3. Warum verspottete
der Hase die Schnecke? — 4. Was wollte der Hase thun, während
(while) die Schnecke sich in der heißen Mittagssonne plagte? —
5. Wann erwachte der Hase von seinem Schläfchen? — 6. Wo war
die Schnecke, als der Hase erwachte? — 7. Was rief die Schnecke
dem Hasen entgegen?

5. Die Grille und die Ameise.

Eine Grille kam bei strenger Kälte[1] zu ihrer
Nachbarin, der Ameise. „Frau Nachbarin,"[2] sagte
sie, „leiht mir doch[3] einige Speise, denn ich habe
Hunger und nichts zu essen." — „Hast du denn nicht

Speise für den Winter gesammelt?“ fragte die Ameise.
— „Ich hatte ja⁴ keine Zeit dazu,“⁵ war die Antwort.
— „Keine Zeit, Frau Grille?“⁶ Was hast du denn im
Sommer⁷ zu thun gehabt?“ — „Ich habe gesungen
und musiziert,“⁸ erwiderte die Grille. — „Nun,“⁹
sprach die Ameise, „da du im Sommer musiziert hast,
so¹⁰ magst du im Winter tanzen. Wer nicht arbeitet,
soll auch nicht essen.“

1. Bei welchem Wetter kam die Grille zur Ameise? — 2. Was
sagte sie zu ihr? — 3. Warum hatte die Grille nichts zu essen?
4. Warum hatte die Grille im Sommer keine Speise gesammelt?
— 5. Was hatte die Grille im Sommer gethan? — 6. Was erwiderte die Ameise der Grille? — 7. Wer soll nicht essen?

6. Der sterbende Löwe.

Ein alter Löwe lag kraftlos¹ vor seiner Höhle und
erwartete den Tod. Die Tiere, deren² Schrecken er
bisher³ gewesen war,⁴ bedauerten ihn nicht; sie freuten
sich vielmehr, daß sie seiner los wurden.⁵ Einige von
ihnen, die er sonst verfolgt hatte, wollten nun ihren
Haß an ihm auslassen. Der arglistige Fuchs kränkte
ihn mit beißenden Reden; der Wolf sagte ihm die
ärgsten Schimpfworte; der Ochse stieß ihn mit den
Hörnern;⁶ das wilde Schwein verwundete ihn mit den
Hauern, und selbst⁷ der träge Esel gab ihm einen
Schlag mit dem Hufe. Das edle⁸ Pferd allein stand⁹

ſchweigend¹⁰ dabei und that ihm nichts, obgleich der Löwe ſeine Mutter zerriſſen hatte. „Willſt du nicht," fragte der Eſel, „dem Löwen auch Eins hinter die Ohren geben?" Das Pferd antwortete: „Ich halte¹² es für niederträchtig, mich an einem Feinde zu rächen,¹³ der mir nicht mehr ſchaden¹⁴ kann."

1. Warum bedauerten die Tiere den Löwen nicht? — 2. Wie ließen die Tiere ihren Haß an dem Löwen aus? — 3. Vergleiche den Löwen von ſonſt und jetzt! — 4. Was ſagte der Eſel zu dem Pferde? — 5. Warum rächte ſich das Pferd nicht an dem Löwen? — 6. Was hatte der Löwe dem Pferde gethan? — 7. Wie heißt die Moral dieſer Fabel?

7. Der höfliche¹ Knabe.

In einem Dorfe nicht weit von Ancona² in Italien lebten einſt arme Bauersleute,³ welche einen Sohn namens⁴ Felix hatten. Dieſer Knabe hatte einen guten Verſtand; weil er aber ſehr arm war, mußte⁵ er die Schweine hüten.

Felix wurde von⁶ ſeinen Eltern immer angehalten, gegen jedermann zuvorkommend, gefällig und freund= lich zu ſein. Die anderen Knaben im Dorfe ver= achteten aber den Schweinehirten und waren unhöflich und grob.

Als Felix eines Tages⁷ ſeine Herde hütete, kam des Weges⁸ ein Barfüßermönch,⁹ der durch den Wald

einen Führer begehrte. Weil es aber schlechtes Wetter
war, so sagten die anderen Knaben in ihrer gewöhn=
lichen Grobheit: „Nein, ich gehe nicht mit!"[10] Da
sprang[11] Felix herbei, grüßte freundlich und bot[12] sich
zum Wegweiser[13] an. Unterwegs erkannte der Mönch
an den klugen Antworten des Knaben den guten Ver=
stand desselben und nahm[14] ihn mit Bewilligung[15] der
Eltern mit in sein Kloster.

Felix studierte jetzt fleißig und trat[16] später in den
Orden ein. Obgleich er bald einer der gelehrtesten
unter den Mönchen wurde, erhob er sich doch nicht
über sie, sondern blieb demütig, höflich und dienst=
fertig. Daher gewannen[17] ihn alle, die ihn kannten,
lieb, und er wurde von einer Ehrenstelle zur anderen
erhoben, bis er endlich Kardinal wurde. Als der
Papst starb, wurde er sogar einstimmig am 24. April
1585[18] zum Papste erwählt.[19] Er hat unter dem
Namen Sixtus V.[20] mit großem Ruhme regiert.

.

1. Wessen Sohn war Felix? — 2. Warum mußte er die
Schweine hüten? — 3. Was lehrten ihn seine Eltern? — 4. Wie
waren die anderen Dorfknaben gegen Felix? — 5. Wer kam einst
des Weges? — 6. Was begehrte der Mönch? — 7. Warum woll=
ten ihn die Knaben nicht durch den Wald führen? — 8. Was that
Felix? — 9. Warum nahm der Mönch den Knaben mit ins
Kloster? — 10. Wie war Felix im Kloster? — 11. Was ist Felix
durch seinen Fleiß und seine Höflichkeit geworden? — 12. Wie
und unter welchem Namen regierte er?

8. Das Hirtenbüblein.

Es war einmal[1] ein Hirtenbüblein, das[2] war wegen seiner weisen Antworten, die es auf alle Fragen gab, weit und breit[3] berühmt. Der König des Landes hörte auch davon, glaubte es nicht und ließ[4] das Büblein kommen. Da sprach er zu ihm: „Kannst du[5] mir auf drei Fragen, die ich dir vorlege,[6] Antwort geben, so will ich dich halten wie mein eigenes Kind." Sprach das Büblein:[7] „Wie lauten die drei Fragen?" Der König sagte: „Wie viel[8] Tropfen Wasser[9] sind in dem Weltmeere?" Das Hirtenbüblein antwortete: „Herr[10] König, laßt[11] alle Flüsse auf der Erde verstopfen, damit kein Tröpfchen mehr daraus ins Meer läuft, das ich nicht erst gezählt habe, so will ich's Euch genau sagen." Der König sprach: „Die andere Frage lautet: „Wie viel Sterne stehen am Himmel?"[12] Das Hirtenbüblein sagte: „Gebt mir einen großen Bogen Papier!"[13] Und dann machte es mit der Feder so viel seine Pünktlein darauf, daß sie kaum zu sehen waren[14] und fast gar nicht[15] zu zählen waren und einem die Augen[16] vergingen, wenn man darauf blickte. Da sprach es: „So viel Sterne stehen am Himmel, wie hier Punkte auf dem Papier; zählt sie nur!" Aber niemand war dazu im stande.[17] Sprach der König: „Die dritte Frage lautet: „Wie viel Sekunden sind in der Ewigkeit?" Das Büblein antwortete: „In Hinterpommern[18] steht der Demantberg,[19] der[20] hat eine Stunde in die Höhe,[21] eine Stunde in die Breite und eine Stunde in die Tiefe; dahin kommt alle hundert Jahre[22] ein Vöglein und wetzt sein Schnäblein daran; und wenn der ganze Berg abgewetzt ist, dann ist[23] die erste Sekunde der Ewigkeit vorbei." Da sagte der König: „Du hast die drei Fragen beantwortet[24] wie ein Weiser,[25] und ich will dich fortan halten wie mein eigenes Kind."

1. Wovon hörte der König? — 2. Wie lauteten die drei Fragen, die der König dem Hirtenbüblein vorlegte? — 3. Wie beantwortete das Hirtenbüblein die erste Frage? die zweite? die dritte? — 4. Waren die Fragen des Königs zu beantworten? — 5. Hat der Knabe die Fragen denn nicht beantwortet? — 6. Wie zeigt der Knabe dem König, daß es unmöglich ist, seine Fragen zu beantworten? — 7. Warum hält der König den Knaben für einen Weisen? — 8. Wie will der König das Büblein halten?

9. Das Wunderkästchen.

Eine Frau hatte in ihrer[2] Haushaltung[3] allerlei[1] Unglücksfälle und ihr[5] Vermögen nahm[4] jährlich ab. Da ging sie in einen Wald zu einem alten Einsiedler,[6] erzählte ihm ihre betrübten Umstände und sagte: „Es geht in meinem Hause nicht mit rechten Dingen zu.[7] Wissen Sie kein Mittel, dem Übel abzuhelfen?"[8]

Der Einsiedler, ein fröhlicher Greis, hieß[9] sie ein

wenig warten, brachte über ein Weilchen⁶ ein kleines
versiegeltes Kästchen und sprach: „Dieses Kästchen
müssen Sie ein Jahr lang⁷ dreimal am Tage und
dreimal in der Nacht⁸ in allen Winkeln des Hau-
ses umhertragen, so wird es besser gehen. Bringen
Sie mir aber übers Jahr⁶ das Kästchen wieder
zurück."

Die gute Hausfrau setzte in das Kästchen ein großes
Vertrauen und trug es fleißig umher. Als sie am
nächsten Tag in den Keller ging, wollte eben ein
Knecht einen Krug Bier⁹ heimlich wegtragen. Als
sie spät abends in die Küche kam, hatten sich¹⁰ die
Mägde einen Kuchen gebacken. Als sie durch die
Stallung ging, standen die Kühe tief im Kot, und die
Pferde hatten statt des Hafers nur Heu und waren
nicht gestriegelt. So hatte sie alle Tage¹¹ einen
Fehler abzustellen.

Als das Jahr um war, ging sie mit dem Kästchen
zum Einsiedler und sagte vergnügt: „Alles geht nun
besser. Lassen Sie mir¹² das Kästchen nur noch ein¹³
Jahr, es enthält ein gar treffliches Mittel." Da
lachte der Einsiedler und sprach: „Das Kästchen kann
ich Ihnen nicht lassen; das Mittel aber, das darin ist,
sollen Sie haben." Er öffnete das Kästchen, und sieh,
es¹⁴ war nichts darin als¹⁵ ein weißes Papier, auf dem
geschrieben stand:

Du mußt, soll's[16] wohl im Hause stehn,[17]
Auf Sparsamkeit und Ordnung sehn.[18]

1. Warum bat die Frau den Einsiedler, ihr zu helfen? (Refer to witchcraft, die Hexerei.) — 2. Aus welchen Worten sehen wir, daß die Frau ihre Unglücksfälle für Hexerei hielt? — 3. Wie half der Einsiedler dem Übel ab? — 4. Warum trug die Frau das Kästchen fleißig umher? — 5. Was sah sie, als sie am nächsten Tage in den Keller ging? — 6. Sind die Mägde sparsam, wenn die Frau selbst nicht auf Sparsamkeit sieht? — 7. Zeigen Sie, daß die Frau noch abergläubisch war, als sie übers Jahr das Kästchen zurückbrachte. — 8. Was enthielt das Kästchen? — 9. Ich glaube, daß die Frau sich etwas schämte, als sie das Papier las. Worüber?

10. Die ewige Bürde.

Der Kalif[1] Hakkam, der die Pracht liebte, wollte die Gärten seines Palastes verschönern und erweitern. Er kaufte alle benachbarten Ländereien[2] und zahlte den Eigentümern so viel dafür, als sie verlangten. Nur eine arme Witwe fand sich,[3] die das Erbteil ihrer Väter aus frommer Gewissenhaftigkeit nicht veräußern wollte und alle Anerbietungen, die man ihr deswegen machte, ausschlug.[4] Den Aufseher der königlichen Gebäude verdroß der Eigensinn dieser Frau; er nahm[5] ihr das kleine Land mit Gewalt[6] weg, und die arme Frau kam weinend zum Richter. Ibn Beschir war eben Kadi[7] der Stadt. Er ließ sich den Fall vortragen und fand ihn bedenklich; denn obschon die Gesetze der Witwe ausdrücklich Recht

gaben,⁹ so war es doch nicht so leicht, einen Fürsten,
der gewohnt war, seinen Willen für die vollkommene
Gerechtigkeit zu halten, zur freiwilligen Erfüllung
eines veralteten Gesetzes zu bewegen. Was that also⁹
der gerechte Kadi? Er sattelte seinen Esel, hing ihm
einen Sack um den Hals¹⁰ und ritt gerade zu der
Zeit¹¹ nach den Gärten des Palastes, als der Kalif sich
eben in dem schönen Gebäude befand, das er auf dem
Erbteile der Witwe erbaut hatte. Die Ankunft des
Kadis mit seinem Esel und Sacke setzte ihn in Verwunderung; und noch mehr erstaunte er, als sich Ibn
Beschir ihm zu Füßen¹² warf und also sagte: „Er-
laube mir, Herr, daß ich diesen Sack mit Erde von
diesem Boden fülle.“ Hakkam gab¹³ es zu. Als der
Sack voll war, bat Ibn Beschir den Kalifen, ihm den
Sack auf den Esel heben¹⁴ zu helfen. Hakkam fand
dies¹⁵ Verlangen noch sonderbarer als alles vorige;
um aber zu sehen, was der Mann vorhatte, griff¹⁶ er
mit¹⁷ an. Allein¹⁸ der Sack war¹⁹ nicht zu bewegen,
und¹ der Kalif sprach: „Die Bürde ist zu schwer,
Kadi.“ „Herr,“ antwortete Ibn Beschir mit edler
Dreistigkeit, „Du findest diese Bürde zu schwer, und
sie enthält doch nur einen kleinen Teil der Erde, die
Du ungerechterweise²⁰ einer armen Witwe genommen
hast! Wie willst Du denn das ganze geraubte Land
tragen können, wenn es der Richter der Welt am

großen Gerichtstage auf Deine Schultern legen wird?"
Der Kalif war betroffen; er lobte die Herzhaftigkeit
und Klugheit des Kadis und gab der Witwe das
Erbe²¹ zurück mit allen Gebäuden, die er darauf
angelegt hatte.

1. Warum kaufte der Kalif alle benachbarten Ländereien? —
2. Warum schlug die Witwe alle Anerbietungen aus? — 3. Was
that der Aufseher der königlichen Gärten deswegen? — 4. Wohin
ging die arme Witwe? — 5. Warum fand Ibn Beschir den Fall
bedenklich? — 6. Was that Ibn Beschir, um der Witwe zu helfen?
— 7. Worüber erstaunte der Kalif? — 8. Worum bat Ibn Beschir den Kalifen? — 9. Was sagte der Kalif über den Sack Erde?
— 10. Wie antwortete ihm der Kadi darauf? — 11. Warum
lobte der Kalif den Kadi? — 12. Was gab der Kalif der Witwe?

11. Der kluge Schäferjunge.

Im siebenjährigen Kriege¹ raubte ein russischer²
Soldat einem Schäferjungen³ ein Schaf von der
Weide. Der Knabe bat inständig, ihm sein Schaf zu
lassen; doch der Soldat war unerbittlich und schleppte⁴
das Tier fort. Da lief der Knabe zu dem Obersten
des Regiments. Dieser versprach, den Soldaten streng
zu bestrafen. „Wenn ich ihn sehe," sagte der Knabe,
„so werde ich ihn gewiß wiedererkennen." Der Oberst
ließ das Regiment antreten. Als es aufgestellt war,
ging der Knabe hinter die Glieder und besah die Leute
von hinten. „Ei," sprach der Oberst, „so wirst du
den Dieb nicht finden. Auf dem Rücken sieht⁵ einer⁶

2

wie der andere aus." „Der, den⁷ ich suche," versetzte der Knabe, „soll anders aussehen." Er ging weiter und zeigte endlich auf⁸ den sechsten Mann im dritten Gliede. „Hier, Herr Oberst," rief er, „habe ich den Schafdieb." Er zog ein Stück Rötel aus der Tasche und fuhr fort:⁹ „Mit diesem Rötel zeichnen wir unsere Schafe, und damit¹⁰ habe ich dem Soldaten¹¹ einen Strich hinten auf die Degenkoppel gemacht, um ihn wiederzuerkennen. Sehen Sie, Herr Oberst, hier ist der Strich." „Bravo,"¹² sagte der Oberst, „der Einfall ist einen Dukaten¹³ wert!" „Aber wer wird mir den geben?" fragte der Knabe. Der Oberst lachte und sprach: „Ich, du Schlaukopf!" Er zog seine Börse und gab dem Knaben das Goldstück.

Der Soldat mußte das Schaf herausgeben und der Oberst wollte ihn streng bestrafen, aber der Knabe legte¹⁴ Fürbitte für ihn ein.

1. Wann war der siebenjährige Krieg? — 2. Was that ein russischer Soldat im siebenjährigen Kriege? — 3. Warum lief der Knabe zum Obersten des Regiments? — 4. Was versprach der Oberst dem Knaben? — 5. Wie fand der Knabe den Soldaten wieder? — 6. Was thun die Schäfer mit dem Rötel? — 7. Warum gab der Oberst dem Knaben einen Dukaten? — 8. Was ist ein Dukaten? — 9. Warum bestrafte der Oberst den Soldaten nicht?

12. Wieland der Schmied.

Wieland¹ war der kunstfertigste Schmied, der je den Hammer geschwungen hat. Über alle Länder war der Ruhm seines Namens verbreitet und wo immer ein kunstvolles Geschmeide oder eine vortreffliche Waffe bewundert wurde, da war es von der Hand Wielands des Schmiedes.

Das Kostbarste und Beste, was[2] er schuf, war das Schwert Mimung.[3] Dieses schmiedete er am Hofe des Königs Neidung im Wettstreit mit dem königlichen Waffenschmiede Amilias. Als es fertig war, prüfte es Wieland auf folgende Weise:[4] er warf eine Flocke Wolle,[5] die drei Fuß[6] dick war, in einen sanft strömenden Teich und ließ sie gegen die Schärfe des Schwertes treiben. Als die Wolle gegen die Schneide[7] glitt, stockte sie keinen Augenblick, denn das Schwert schnitt[8] sie glatt durch.

Wohlzufrieden mit der Probe begab sich Wieland an den Hof, wo der Wettstreit mit Amilias stattfinden sollte. Da stand des Königs Schmied in einer glänzenden Rüstung, die er so hart gestählt hatte, daß alle Schwerter auf derselben zerschellten wie Glas. Höhnend forderte[9] er Wieland auf, sein Schwert auf seinem Helme zu prüfen. Da legte Wieland Mimungs Schneide auf den Helm und drückte leise. „Nun, fühlst du etwas?" fragte er. Amilias entgegnete: „Hau[10] nur zu aus Leibeskräften,[11] mein Helm bleibt dennoch unversehrt." Da drückte Wieland stärker, und die Klinge glitt durch den Helm und den Panzer

herab bis[12] auf den Gürtel. „Fühlst du jetzt etwas?"
fragte Wieland. „Mir war,[13] als wenn[14] mir ein
Tropfen Wasser am Leibe[15] heruntergelaufen wäre."[16]
„So schüttel[17] dich einmal!"[18] rief Wieland. Amilias
schüttelte sich, da fiel nach beiden Seiten ein halber[19]
Ritter ins Gras: Wielands Schwert hatte ihn mitten
durchgeschnitten.

Seit diesem Tage[20] war Mimung das berühmteste
Schwert, das je von einem Helden getragen wurde.

1. Wer war Wieland? — 2. Was schmiedete er? — 3. Wo
schuf er das kostbare Schwert Mimung? — 4. Wie prüfte Wieland
die Schneide des Schwertes? — 5. Wer war Amilias? — 6. Was
hatte Amilias geschmiedet? — 7. Wozu forderte Amilias seinen
Gegner auf? — 8. Was that Wieland? — 9. Was antwortete
Amilias auf Wielands Frage? — 10. Was geschah, als Wieland
stärker drückte? — 11. Was fühlte Amilias, als ihm das Schwert
durch Helm und Panzer glitt? — 12. Was geschah, als Amilias
sich schüttelte?

13. Siegfried.[1]

In den Niederlanden[2] wohnte in uralter[3] Zeit ein
König, namens Siegmund, der weithin berühmt war
durch seine große Macht. Dieser hatte einen Sohn,
namens Siegfried, einen Knaben von unbändiger
Kraft, dessen ganzes Trachten dahin ging,[4] in die
Fremde zu ziehen, um Abenteuer zu bestehen. Endlich
gab[5] der König dem Wunsche seines Sohnes nach und
ließ ihn ziehen.

Siegfried kam bald in ein Dorf, das vor einem Walde lag. Dort verdang er sich bei einem Schmied,[6] um Waffen schmieden zu lernen.[7] Aber er schlug so gewaltig auf das Eisen, daß dieses zersprang,[8] und der Ambos in die Erde getrieben ward.[9] Der Meister fürchtete[10] sich deshalb vor ihm und suchte sich des wilden Gesellen wieder zu entledigen.[11] Er schickte ihn daher in den nahen Wald zu einem Köhler; aber unterwegs mußte[12] Siegfried an der Höhle eines greulichen Drachens vorbei, und dieser, dachte der Meister, werde[13] den jungen Helden töten. Wirklich fuhr[14] der Drache auf den nichts ahnenden Wanderer los, aber Siegfried wehrte sich und erschlug ihn. Darauf ging er weiter und geriet bald in eine Wildnis,[15] in welcher es von Drachen, Kröten und anderem giftigem Gewürm[16] wimmelte. Ohne sich zu besinnen,[17] riß er eine Menge der stärksten Bäume aus der Erde, warf sie auf die Untiere[18] und zündete[19] dann den ganzen Holzstoß an. Von der Glut begann die Hornhaut der Ungetüme[20] zu schmelzen und ein Strom von dieser Masse floß unter[21] dem brennenden Haufen hervor. Neugierig tauchte Siegfried seinen Finger hinein,[22] und siehe da, als er erkaltet war, hatte ihn eine undurchdringliche Hornschicht überzogen.[23] Da bestrich sich der Held den ganzen Leib aus diesem trägen Strom und ward dadurch ganz mit

Horn überzogen, so daß ihn kein Schwert verwunden konnte; nur zwischen den Schultern blieb auf dem Rücken eine Stelle, die er nicht erreichen konnte. An dieser sollte er frühzeitig den Tod empfangen.

1. Wer war Siegfried? — 2. Wonach trachtete Siegfried? — 3. Wollte sein Vater ihn anfangs ziehen lassen? — 4. Was that er in dem Dorfe, in das er kam? — 5. Warum fürchtete sich der Schmied vor ihm? — 6. Wie suchte sich der Schmied des wilden Gesellen zu entledigen? — 7. Wurde Siegfried von dem Drachen getötet? — 8. Wie war es in der Wildnis, in die Siegfried kam, als er den Drachen erschlagen hatte? — 9. Was that Siegfried, um sich gegen das giftige Gewürm zu wehren? — 10. Wie ward Siegfried unverwundbar? — 11. Warum blieb er zwischen den Schultern verwundbar? — 12. An welchen griechischen Helden erinnert uns Siegfried, und warum?

14. Der Edelknabe des Königs.

Ein berühmter preußischer General war in seiner Jugend Edelknabe an dem Hofe Friedrichs des Großen. Er hatte keinen Vater mehr, und seine Mutter nährte sich in ihrem Witwenstande kümmerlich. Als guter Sohn[1] wünschte er sie zu unterstützen, aber von seinem Gehalte konnte er nichts entbehren.[2] Doch fand er endlich ein Mittel, etwas für sie zu erwerben. Jede Nacht mußte einer von den Edelknaben in dem Zimmer vor dem Schlafgemach des Königs wachen, um diesem aufzuwarten,[3] wenn er etwas verlangte. Manchem war dies[4] beschwerlich, und sie übertrugen daher, wenn

die Reihe sie traf,⁵ ihre Wachen gern⁶ an andere. Der
arme Page⁷ fing an, diese Wachen für andere zu über=
nehmen; sie wurden ihm vergütet, und das Geld,
welches er dafür erhielt, schickte er dann seiner Mutter.

Einst konnte der König in der Nacht nicht schlafen
und wollte sich etwas vorlesen lassen.⁸ Er klingelte,
er rief; allein es kam niemand. Endlich stand er
selbst auf und ging in das Nebenzimmer, um zu sehen,
ob kein Page da wäre?⁹ Hier fand er den guten
Jüngling, der die Wache übernommen hatte, am
Tische sitzen.¹⁰ Vor ihm lag ein Brief an seine
Mutter, den er zu schreiben angefangen hatte; allein
er war über¹¹ demselben eingeschlafen. Der König
schlich herbei und las den Anfang des Briefes, welcher
so lautete: „Meine beste, geliebteste Mutter! Jetzt ist
es schon die dritte Nacht, daß ich für Geld Wache
habe. Beinahe kann ich es nicht mehr aushalten.
Indes freue ich mich, daß ich nun wieder zehn Thaler
für Dich¹² verdient habe, welche ich Dir hiermit schicke.“
Gerührt über das gute Herz des Jünglings läßt der
König ihn schlafen, geht in sein Zimmer, holt zwei
Rollen Dukaten, steckt ihm in jede Tasche eine und
legt sich wieder zu Bette.

Als der Edelknabe erwachte und das Geld in seinen
Taschen fand, konnte er wohl denken, woher es ge=
kommen sei.¹³ Er freute sich zwar darüber, weil er

nun seine Mutter noch mehr unterstützen konnte; doch erschrak er auch zugleich, daß der König ihn schlafend[14] gefunden hatte. Am Morgen, sobald er zum Könige kam, bat[15] er demütig um Vergebung wegen seines Dienstfehlers und dankte ihm für das Geschenk. Der König lobte seine kindliche Liebe, ernannte[16] ihn sogleich zum Offizier und schenkte ihm noch eine Summe Geldes, um sich alles anzuschaffen, was er zu seiner neuen Stelle brauchte. Der treffliche Sohn stieg hernach immer[17] höher und diente[18] den preußischen Königen als tapferer General bis in sein hohes Alter.

1. Wie kam der Knabe an den Hof des Königs? — 2. Welchen Dienst hatten die Edelknaben während der Nacht? — 3. Warum übernahm der Page die Wachen für andere? — 4. Warum wollte sich der König etwas vorlesen lassen? — 5. Was sah der König, als er in das Nebenzimmer kam? — 6. Was enthielt der Brief des Edelknaben an seine Mutter? — 7. Wie belohnte der König den Knaben für seine kindliche Liebe? — 8. Worüber freute sich der Edelknabe? — 9. Was that der Edelknabe am Morgen, als er zum König kam? — 10. Beendigen Sie den Brief des Edelknaben an seine Mutter.

15. Wie Rübezahl[1] Holz fahren hilft.

Ein armer Bauersmann hatte sich[2] ein wenig Holz im Gebirge zusammengelesen, in der Hoffnung, es bei guter Schneebahn[3] bequem hinunter zu bringen. Da der Winter aber strenge war und dabei[4] wenig

Schnee fiel, mußte er mit Weib und Kindern große
Kälte ausstehn. In solcher Not ging er in den
Wald, um etwas Holz nach Hause zu schaffen. Wie
er so recht in Gedanken⁵ dastand und keinen Rat
wußte, das Holz den Berg hinunter zu bringen, kam
unverhofft ein Mann mit einem Schlitten auf ihn zu⁶
und fragte, was ihm fehle.⁷ Der Bauer klagte seine
Not. „Seid ohne Sorge," entgegnete Rübezahl —
denn dies war der andere — „helft nur⁸ das Holz auf
den Schlitten packen, dann will ich euch hinunter
helfen." Da luden sie beide Schlitten, Rübezahls
und des Bauern, voll auf. Rübezahl hieß ihn ge=
trost bergab fahren und folgte ihm nach. Das ging
wie der Blitz; ehe sich's der Bauer versah,⁹ waren sie
unten. Rübezahl half ihm den Schlitten bis¹⁰ vor
das Haus schieben, trat in die Stube und nahm für=
lieb mit dem, was ihm die guten Leute, die an dem
vielen Holze große Freude hatten, bereitwillig auf=
trugen. Der Bauer gab ihm auch einige Groschen¹¹
für seine Mühe. Zwei hübsche Kinder, welche in der
Stube umhersprangen, gefielen¹² Rübezahl besonders
wohl. Er rief das eine, einen muntern Knaben,
freundlich zu sich, zog ein paar Kügelchen aus der
Tasche und sagte: „Sieh, was ich dir zum Spielen¹³
schenke!" Der Knabe griff beherzt zu, und weil das
andere Kind so verlangend darnach¹⁴ blickte, aber nicht

heranzukommen wagte, warf ihm Rübezahl gleichfalls
so[15] ein paar[16] Kügelchen in den Schoß. Darauf
nahm er Abschied und zog mit seinem Schlitten dem
Gebirge zu.[17] Nach einer guten Weile, als die Eltern
eine von den kleinen Kugeln in die Hand nahmen und
näher betrachteten, entdeckten sie, daß es lauter gediegenes Gold war. Da wurden sie recht von Herzen
froh, denn sie waren blutarm[18] und konnten nun von
dem Golde eine schöne Zeit[19] haushalten. Ihre
Freude war so groß, daß sie das unverhoffte Glück sogar ihrem Nachbar erzählten, einem geizigen Manne,
der ihnen nie in der Not geholfen hatte. Das machte[20]
dem Geizigen Lust, auf gleicher Weise zu solchem
Glücke zu gelangen. Am andern Morgen[21] ging er
gleichfalls nach dem Gebirge, um sich Holz zu holen.
Doch weil ihm niemand zu Hilfe[22] kommen wollte, so
mußte er zuletzt seinen Schlitten ganz allein und ledig
wieder nach Hause[23] schleppen.

1. Was hatte ein armer Bauersmann gethan? — 2. Warum
mußte er mit Weib und Kind große Kälte ausstehen? — 3. Warum
stand der Bauer in Gedanken da? — 4. Wer kam unverhofft des
Weges? — 5. Was sagte Rübezahl zu dem Bauern? — 6. Wie
ging es den Berg hinunter? — 7. Warum gab der Bauer Rübezahl einige Groschen? — 8. Wie viele Kinder hatte der Bauer? —
9. Was schenkte Rübezahl den Kindern? — 10. Warum wollte
das kleine Mädchen ihm die Kügelchen nicht aus der Hand nehmen?
— 11. Was entdeckten die Eltern nach einer Weile? — 12. Erzählen Sie, was dem geizigen Nachbarn geschah?

16. Der Star von Segringen.[1]

Selbst[2] einem Star kann es nützlich[3] sein, wenn er etwas gelernt hat, wie viel mehr einem Menschen. — Der Barbier in Segringen hatte einen Star, und der Lehrjunge[4] gab ihm Unterricht im Sprechen. Der Star lernte nicht nur alle Wörter, die ihm sein Sprachmeister aufgab,[5] sondern er ahmte zuletzt auch selber nach, was er von seinem Herrn hörte, z. B.:[6] „So, so, lala;"[7] oder "Par Compagnie"[8] (das heißt so viel als in Gesellschaft mit anderen); oder „Wie Gott will;" oder „Du Dolpatsch."[9] So titulierte[10] er[11] nämlich den Lehrjungen, wenn er das Schermesser am Rücken abzog, anstatt an der Schneide, oder wenn er ein Arzneiglas[12] zerbrach. Alle diese Redensarten lernte nach und nach[13] der Star auch. Da nun täglich viele Leute im Haus waren, so gab's manchmal viel zu lachen, wenn die Gäste mit einander ein Gespräch führten, und der Star auch eines von seinen Wörtlein drein[14] warf, daß sich dazu schickte, als wenn[15] er den Verstand davon hätte, und manchmal, wenn ihm der Lehrjunge rief: „Hansel,[16] was machst du?" antwortete er: „Du Dolpatsch," und alle Leute in der Nachbarschaft wußten von dem Hansel zu erzählen. Eines Tages aber, als ihm die beschnittenen Flügel wieder gewachsen waren, und das Fenster offen

war, und das Wetter schön, da dachte der Star: Ich
hab'[17] jetzt schon so viel gelernt, daß ich in der Welt
fortkommen kann, und husch zum Fenster hinaus.
Weg war er.   Sein erster Flug ging ins Feld, wo er
sich unter eine Gesellschaft anderer Vögel mischte, und
als sie aufflogen, flog er mit ihnen, denn er dachte:
Sie wissen die Gelegenheit hier zu Land[18] besser als
ich.   Aber sie flogen unglücklicherweise alle miteinan-
der in ein Garn.   Als der Vogelsteller kommt[19] und
sieht, was[20] er für einen Fang gethan hat, nimmt er
einen Vogel nach dem andern behutsam heraus, dreht
ihm den Hals um, und wirft ihn auf den Boden.
Als er aber die mörderischen Finger wieder nach
einem Gefangenen ausstreckte, und denkt an nichts,
schrie der Gefangene: „Ich bin der Barbier von
Segringen"; als wenn[15] er wüßte, was ihn retten
muß.   Der Vogelsteller erschrak anfänglich, als wenn
es hier nicht mit rechten Dingen zuginge,[21] nachher
aber, als er sich erholt hatte, konnte er kaum vor
Lachen[22] zu Atem kommen;[23] und als er sagte: „Ei,
Hansel, hier habe ich dich nicht gesucht, wie kommst du
in meine Schlinge?" da antwortete der Hansel: "Par
Compagnie." Also[24] brachte der Vogelsteller den Star
seinem Herrn wieder, und bekam ein gutes Fanggeld.
Der Barbier aber erwarb sich damit einen guten Zu-
spruch, denn jeder wollte den merkwürdigen Hansel sehen.

1. Was ist allen Leuten nützlich? — 2. Was lernte der Star des Barbiers in Segringen? — 3. Wann nannte der Meister den Lehrjungen einen Dolpatsch? — 4. Worüber gab es im Hause des Barbiers viel zu lachen? — 5. Warum hatte der Barbier dem Star die Flügel beschnitten? — 6. Was dachte der Star eines Tages — 7. Wohin flog er? — 8. Warum flog er mit den anderen Vögeln? — 9. Was geschah den Vögeln? — 10. Was that der Vogelsteller? — 11. Worüber erschrak der Vogelsteller? — 12. Drehte der Vogelsteller dem Star auch den Hals um?

17. Die weiße Maus.

Auf eine merkwürdige und noch immer¹ nicht ganz aufgeklärte² Weise kam eine weiße Maus zu Tode,³ welche mein jüngster Bruder Paul in seiner Kindheit zärtlich pflegte. Das hübsche Tier war äußerst zahm und wohnte in einem kleinen Holzkasten mit Drahtgitter, der auf dem geräumigen Schreibtisch meiner Brüder stand. Dieser Käfig war nie verschlossen und das zierliche Geschöpf lief den ganzen Tag auf dem Schreibtisch zwischen den Büchern herum, ohne jemals daran zu denken,⁴ seine Exkursionen⁵ weiter auszudehnen. Eines Tages wurde eine wilde, schwarze Maus gefangen und trotz des Protestes⁶ meiner Mutter dem kleinen, weißen Prinzen zugesellt.⁷ Die Tierchen schienen sich gut zu vertragen, allein am andern Morgen war ein Loch in den Käfig genagt und die schwarze Maus verschwunden. Seit dieser

Zeit war die weiße ganz verwandelt. Zwar von ihrer Zahmheit hatte sie nichts eingebüßt; sie duckte sich wie immer geduldig zusammen und stieß ein zartes Warnungsquietschen aus, wenn man sie in die Hand nehmen wollte, allein eine starke Unruhe hatte sich ihrer bemächtigt;[8] sie lief auf dem Tische schnüffelnd und suchend umher und probierte mehrfach über den Rand in die Tiefe zu gelangen. Eines Tages war sie verschwunden, jedoch nicht lange. Einige Zeit, nachdem ihre Abwesenheit bemerkt war, entstand ein erbärmlicher Lärm unter dem Fußboden des Zimmers, ein Gequietsch und Gerappel, wie es bei Familienzwistigkeiten unter den Mäusen gebräuchlich ist, erhob sich, und plötzlich kam aus dem Mauseloch hinter dem Ofen die weiße Maus in großer Angst hervorgestürzt.[9] Sie war offenbar herausgeworfen worden.

Einige Tage hielt sie sich nun ruhig auf ihrem Tische, jedoch der Friede ihres Gemüts war gestört. Meine Schwester behauptete, die Maus säße[10] jeden Nach=mittag am Rande des Tisches auf Zumpts Gram=matik[11] und seufze — die roten Augen sehnsüchtig auf das Mauseloch gerichtet. Und es kam eine Zeit, wo[12] die Sehnsucht die Vorsicht überwog, und wo sie wiederum verschwunden war. Aber diesmal erhob sich ein Lärm, noch viel entsetzlicher als das erste Mal,

und am Ende kam das Tierchen mühsam aus dem
Mauseloch hervor und blieb erschöpft auf dem Fuß=
boden liegen. In seinem rosigen Schnäuzchen hatte
es einen Biß und auf dem weißen Sammetfell standen
rote Blutflecke. Man[13] legte es auf Watte in eine
Schachtel und flößte ihm Milch ein. Am andern
Morgen lebte es noch, aber gegen Mittag ward es
matter und matter, reckte sich noch einmal und ver=
schied;[14] mein Bruder sagte, an seinen Wunden, meine
Schwester aber behauptete, an gebrochenem Herzen.

In seiner Sterbeschachtel ward der weiße Prinz im
Garten feierlich begraben, und mein Bruder errichtete auf
seinem Grabe ein Denkmal mit der Inschrift: „Hier
ruhet tief betrauert von Paul Seidel seine weiße Maus.“

1. Wie kam die weiße Maus zu Tode? — 2. Worin wohnte das
Tierchen? — 3. Was that die Maus den ganzen Tag? — 4. Was
that man mit der wilden Maus, die gefangen wurde? — 5. Blieb
die wilde Maus in dem Kasten? — 6. Wie war die weiße Maus
von nun an? — 7. Wie zeigte sich die Unruhe der Maus? —
8. Was hörte man einige Zeit nach ihrem Verschwinden? —
9. Was geschah plötzlich? — 10. Blieb die Maus jetzt auf ihrem
Tische? — 11. Wie kam das arme Tierchen das zweite Mal aus
dem Mauseloche hervor? — 12. Was that man für das arme
Tierchen? — 13. Woran starb die Maus? — 14. Wo wurde sie
begraben? — 15. Was that Paul?

18. Rotkäppchen.

Es war einmal[1] ein kleines, liebes Mädchen, das[2]
hatte jedermann gern, der es nur ansah, am aller=

liebſten⁵ aber ſeine Großmutter; die wußte gar nicht,
was ſie alles dem Kinde geben ſollte.⁴ Einmal
ſchenkte ſie ihm ein Käppchen von⁵ rotem Sammet,
und weil ihm das ſo wohl ſtand,⁶ und es nichts
anderes mehr tragen wollte, hieß es nur das Rot=
käppchen.⁷ Da ſagte einmal ſeine Mutter zu ihm:
„Komm, Rotkäppchen, da haſt du ein Stück Kuchen⁸
und eine Flaſche Wein, die bring der Großmutter hin=
aus, ſie iſt krank und ſchwach und wird ſich daran
laben. Sei aber hübſch artig⁹ und grüß ſie von mir,
geh' auch ordentlich und lauf nicht vom Wege ab, ſonſt
fällſt du und zerbrichſt die Flaſche, dann hat die
kranke Großmutter nichts.“

Rotkäppchen ſagte: „Ich will ſchon¹⁰ alles gut aus=
richten,“ und gab der Mutter die Hand darauf. Die
Großmutter aber wohnte draußen im Wald, eine
halbe Stunde vom Dorf. Wie¹¹ nun Rotkäppchen in
den Wald kam, begegnete ihm¹² der Wolf. Rotkäpp=
chen aber wußte nicht, was das für ein böſes Tier war,
und fürchtete¹³ ſich nicht vor ihm. „Guten Tag,
Rotkäppchen,“ ſprach er. „Schönen Dank,¹⁴ Wolf.“
„Wo hinaus¹⁵ ſo früh, Rotkäppchen?“ „Zur Groß=
mutter.“ „Was trägſt du unter der Schürze?“
„Kuchen und Wein, geſtern haben wir gebacken, da
ſoll ſich die kranke, ſchwache Großmutter etwas zu gut
thun¹⁶ und ſich damit ſtärken.“ „Rotkäppchen, wo

wohnt deine Großmutter?" „Noch eine gute Viertel=
stunde weiter im Wald, unter den drei großen Eich=
bäumen, da steht ihr Haus, unten sind die Nußhecken,
das wirst du ja[17] wissen," sagte Rotkäppchen. Der
Wolf dachte bei sich:[18] „Das junge, zarte Mädchen,
das ist ein guter, fetter Bissen für dich; wie fängst
du's an, daß du den kriegst?" Da ging er ein Weil=
chen neben Rotkäppchen her; dann sprach er: „Rot=
käppchen, sieh einmal[19] die schönen Blumen, die im
Walde stehen, warum guckst du nicht um dich; ich
glaube, du hörst gar nicht, wie die Vöglein so lieblich
singen. Du gehst ja für dich hin,[20] als wie[21] zur
Schule, und es ist so lustig draußen im Walde."

Rotkäppchen schlug die Augen auf, und als es sah,
wie die Sonne durch die Bäume hin und her sprang
und alles voll[22] schöner Blumen stand, dachte es:
„Ei! wenn ich der Großmutter einen Strauß mit=
bringe, der wird ihr auch lieb sein; es ist noch früh,
daß ich doch[23] zu rechter Zeit ankomme," — und es
sprang in den Wald und suchte Blumen.

Der Wolf aber ging geradeswegs[24] nach dem Haus
der Großmutter und klopfte an die Thüre. Wer ist
draußen? „Rotkäppchen, das bringt Kuchen und
Wein, mach' auf." „Drück' nur auf die Klinke," rief
die Großmutter, „ich bin zu schwach und kann nicht
aufstehen." Der Wolf drückte auf die Klinke, trat

3

hinein und ging, ohne ein Wort zu sprechen,²⁵ an das
Bett der Großmutter und verschluckte sie. Da
nahm er ihre Kleider, that sie an, setzte ihre Haube
auf, legte sich in ihr Bett und zog die Vorhänge vor.

Rotkäppchen aber war derweil nach den Blumen
gelaufen, und als es so viele hatte, daß es keine mehr
tragen konnte, fiel ihm die Großmutter wieder ein,
und es machte sich auf den Weg²⁶ zu ihr. Es wun=
derte sich, daß die Thüre aufstand, und wie es in die
Stube trat, so kam es ihm so seltsam darin vor, daß
es dachte: „Ei, wie ängstlich wird mir's heut zu
Mut,²⁷ und ich bin sonst so gern bei der Großmutter!"
Es sprach: „Guten Morgen," bekam aber keine Ant=
wort. Darauf ging es ans Bett und zog die Vor=
hänge zurück: da lag die Großmutter und hatte die
Haube tief ins Gesicht gezogen und sah so wunderlich
aus. „Ei, Großmutter, was hast du für große
Ohren!" „Daß ich dich besser hören kann." „Ei,
Großmutter, was hast du für große Augen!" „Daß
ich dich besser sehen kann." „Ei, Großmutter, was
hast du für große Hände!" „Daß ich dich besser
packen kann." „Aber, Großmutter, was hast du für
ein entsetzlich großes Maul!" „Daß ich dich besser
fressen kann." Und wie der Wolf das gesagt hatte,
that er einen Satz²⁸ aus dem Bett auf das arme Rot=
käppchen und verschlang es.

Wie der Wolf sein Gelüsten gestillt hatte, legte er sich wieder ins Bett, schlief ein und fing an überlaut zu schnarchen. Der Jäger ging eben vorbei und dachte bei sich: „Wie kann die alte Frau so schnarchen, du mußt einmal nachsehen, ob ihr etwas fehlt.“[29] Da trat er in die Stube, und wie er vor das Bett kam, so lag der Wolf darin. „Finde ich dich endlich, alter Graukopf, ich habe dich lange gesucht.“ Nun wollte er seine Büchse anlegen, da fiel ihm ein: „der Wolf hat vielleicht die Großmutter gefressen, und ich kann sie noch retten,“ und schoß nicht, sondern nahm eine Schere und schnitt dem schlafenden Wolf den Bauch auf. Wie er ein paar Schnitte gethan hatte, da sah er das rote Käppchen leuchten, und noch ein paar Schnitte, da sprang das Mädchen heraus und rief: „Ach, wie war ich erschrocken, wie war’s so dunkel[30] in dem Wolfe!“ Und dann kam die alte Großmutter auch noch lebendig[31] heraus und konnte kaum atmen. Rotkäppchen holte nun geschwind große Steine, damit füllten sie dem Wolf den Leib, und wie er aufwachte, wollte er fortspringen, aber die Steine waren so schwer, daß er gleich niedersank und sich tot fiel.[32]

Da waren alle drei vergnügt; der Jäger nahm den Pelz des Wolfes, die Großmutter aß den Kuchen und trank den Wein, den Rotkäppchen gebracht hatte, und Rotkäppchen dachte bei sich: „Du willst nie wieder allein vom Wege ab in den Wald laufen, wenn dir's die Mutter verboten hat."

1. Wie bekam das kleine Mädchen den Namen Rotkäppchen? — 2. Was sagte die Mutter einmal zu ihm? — 3. Was trug sich im Walde zu? — 4. Wo wohnte Rotkäppchens Großmutter? 5. Was dachte der Wolf bei sich? — 6. Wie ging Rotkäppchen durch den Wald? — 7. Was sah es, als es die Augen aufschlug? — 8. Was that der Wolf, während Rotkäppchen im Walde Blumen pflückte? — 9. Wann fiel dem Mädchen die Großmutter wieder ein? — 10. Wie war Rotkäppchen zu Mut, als es in die Stube trat? — 11. Erzähle was in der Stube geschah! — 12. Was that der Wolf als er sein Gelüsten gestillt hatte? — 13. Was dachte der Jäger bei sich, als er das laute Schnarchen hörte? — 14. Warum schoß der Jäger den Wolf nicht tot? — 15. Auf welche Weise wurden Rotkäppchen und die alte Großmutter gerettet? — 16. Was wollte Rotkäppchen nie wieder thun?

19. Baron von Münchhausen.[1]

In Rußland hatte ich einmal einen merkwürdigen Vorfall mit einer Kette Hühner. Ich war ausgegangen, um eine neue Flinte[2] zu probieren, und hatte meinen kleinen Vorrat von Hagel ganz und gar[3] verschossen, als wider alles Vermuten vor meinen Füßen eine Flucht Hühner aufging. Der Wunsch, einige derselben abends auf meinem Tische zu sehen, brachte mich auf einen Einfall,[4] von dem Sie, meine Herren, auf mein Wort, im Falle der Not Gebrauch machen können. Sobald ich gesehen hatte, wo sich die Hühner niederließen, lud ich hurtig mein Gewehr,

und ſetzte ſtatt des Schrotes[5] den Ladſtock auf, den ich,
ſo gut ſich's in der Eile thun ließ,[6] an dem obern
Ende etwas zuſpitzte.   Nun ging ich auf die Hühner
zu, drückte, ſo wie[7] ſie aufflogen, ab, und hatte das
Vergnügen zu ſehen, daß mein Ladſtock mit ſieben
Stück,[8] die ſich wohl wundern mochten, ſo früh am
Spieße vereinigt zu werden, in einiger Entfernung
allmählich herunterſank. — Wie geſagt,[9] man muß
ſich nur in der Welt zu helfen wiſſen.

Ein anderes Mal ſtieß[10] mir in einem anſehnlichen
Walde von Rußland ein wunderſchöner, ſchwarzer
Fuchs auf. Es wäre Schade geweſen,[11] ſeinen koſtbaren
Pelz mit einem Kugel= oder Schrotſchuſſe[12] zu durch=
löchern. Herr Reineke[13] ſtand dicht bei einem Baume.
Augenblicklich zog ich meine Kugel aus dem Laufe,
lud dafür[14] einen tüchtigen Nagel in mein Gewehr,
feuerte, und traf ſo glücklich, daß ich ſeine Lunte feſt
an den Baum nagelte. Nun ging ich ruhig zu ihm,
nahm mein Weidmeſſer, gab ihm einen Kreuzſchnitt
über's Geſicht, griff nach meiner Peitſche und kar=
batſchte[15] ihn ſo artig aus ſeinem ſchönen Pelze her=
aus, daß es eine wahre Luſt und ein rechtes Wunder
zu ſehen war.

Zufall und gutes Glück machen[16] oft manchen
Fehler wieder gut. Davon erlebte ich bald ein Bei=
ſpiel, als ich mitten im tiefſten Walde einen wilden

Frischling und eine Bache dicht hinter einander her=
traben sah. Meine Kugel hatte gefehlt. Gleichwohl
lief der Frischling vorn ganz allein[17] weg, und die
Bache blieb stehen, ohne Bewegung, als ob[18] sie an
den Boden fest genagelt gewesen wäre. Wie ich das
Ding näher untersuchte, so fand ich, daß es eine blinde
Bache war, die ihres Frischlings Schwänzlein im
Rachen hielt, um von ihm aus kindlicher Pflicht für=
baß[19] geleitet zu werden. Da nun meine Kugel
zwischen beide hindurch gefahren war, so hatte sie
diesen Leitzaum zerrissen, wovon die alte Bache das
eine Ende noch immer[20] kaute. Da nun ihr Leiter
sie nicht weiter vorwärts gezogen hatte, so war sie
stehen geblieben. Ich ergriff daher das übrig ge=
bliebene Endchen[21] von des Frischlings Schwanze,
und leitete daran das alte, hülflose Tier ganz ohne
Mühe und Widerstand nach Hause.

So[22] fürchterlich diese wilden Bachen oft sind, so
sind die Keiler doch weit grausamer und gefährlicher.
Ich traf einst einen im Walde an, als ich unglücklicher
Weise weder auf Angriff noch Verteidigung gefaßt[23]
war. Mit genauer Not[24] konnte ich noch hinter
einen Baum schlüpfen, als die wütende Bestie aus
Leibeskräften[25] einen Seitenhieb nach mir[26] that.
Dafür[27] fuhren aber auch seine Hauer dergestalt in
den Baum hinein, daß er weder im stande war, sie

sogleich wieder herauszuziehen, noch den Hieb zu wiederholen. — Haha! dachte ich, nun wollen wir dich bald kriegen! — Flugs nahm ich einen Stein, hämmerte noch vollends ·damit darauf los, und nietete seine Hauer dergestalt um, daß er ganz und gar nicht[28] wieder loskommen konnte. So mußte er sich denn gedulden, bis ich vom nächsten Dorfe Karren und Stricke herbeigeholt hatte, um ihn lebendig und wohlbehalten nach Hause zu schaffen, welches auch ganz vortrefflich von statten ging."[29]

1. Warum war Münchhausen ausgegangen? — 2. Welchen Wunsch hatte der Baron, als er die Flucht Hühner sah? — 3. Warum lud er seine Flinte nicht mit Hagel? — 4. Was that er mit dem Ladstock, ehe er sein Gewehr damit lud? — 5. Wie viel Hühner schoß er mit dem Ladstock? — 6. Worüber mochten sich die Hühner wohl wundern? — 7. Was stieß dem Baron ein anderes Mal auf? — 8. Warum lud er den Nagel in sein Gewehr? — 9. Wie traf er den Fuchs? — 10. Was that er, um den Pelz zu bekommen? — 11. Wovon erlebte Münchhausen einmal ein Beispiel? — 12. Was sah er mitten im Walde? — 13. Hatte seine Kugel getroffen? — 14. Wie blieb die Bache stehen? — 15. Was fand er, wie er das Ding näher untersuchte? 16. Was hatte seine Kugel gethan? — 17. Auf welche Weise brachte er die Bache nach Hause? — 18. Was für ein Tier ist ein Keiler? — 19. Warum schlüpfte Münchhausen hinter den Baum? — 20. Wozu war der Keiler nicht im stande? — 21. Was that jetzt der Baron?

20. Dornröschen.[1]

Vor Zeiten[2] war[3] ein König und eine Königin, die sprachen jeden Tag: „Ach, wenn wir doch ein Kind

hätten!"[4] und kriegten immer keins. Da trug sich's
zu, daß sie ein Mädchen bekamen,[5] das war so schön,
daß der König vor Freude sich nicht zu lassen wußte[6]
und ein großes Fest anstellte. Er lud nicht blos seine
Verwandten,[7] Freunde und Bekannten, sondern auch
die weisen Frauen[8] dazu ein, damit[9] sie dem Kinde
hold und gewogen wären. Es waren ihrer dreizehn[10]
in seinem Reiche; weil er aber nur zwölf goldene
Teller hatte, von welchen sie essen sollten, so mußte
eine von ihnen daheim bleiben. Das Fest ward mit
aller Pracht gefeiert, und als es zu Ende war, be-
schenkten die weisen Frauen das Kind mit ihren
Wundergaben; die eine mit Tugend, die andere mit
Schönheit, die dritte mit Reichtum, und so mit Allem,
was auf der Welt zu wünschen ist.[11] Als elfe[12] ihre
Sprüche eben gethan hatten,[13] trat plötzlich die dreizehnte herein. Sie wollte sich dafür rächen, daß sie
nicht eingeladen war, und ohne Jemand zu grüßen
oder nur[14] anzusehen, rief sie mit lauter Stimme:
„Die Königstochter soll sich in ihrem fünfzehnten
Jahre an einer Spindel stechen und tot hinfallen."
Und ohne ein Wort weiter zu sprechen, kehrte sie sich
um und verließ den Saal. Alle waren erschrocken, da
trat die zwölfte hervor, die ihren Wunsch noch übrig
hatte; und weil sie den bösen Spruch nicht aufheben,
sondern ihn nur mildern konnte, so sagte sie: „Es soll

aber kein Tod sein, sondern nur ein hundertjähriger, tiefer Schlaf, in welchen die Königstochter fällt."

Der König, der sein liebes Kind vor dem Unglück gern bewahren wollte,[15] ließ den Befehl ausgehen,[16] daß alle Spindeln im ganzen Königreiche verbrannt werden sollten.[17] An dem Mädchen[18] aber wurden die Gaben der weisen Frauen sämmtlich erfüllt, denn es war so schön, sittsam, freundlich und verständig, daß es jedermann, der es ansah, lieb haben mußte. Es geschah, daß an dem Tage, wo[19] es gerade fünfzehn Jahre alt ward, der König und die Königin nicht zu Hause waren, und das Mädchen ganz allein im Schlosse zurückblieb. Da ging es allerorten[20] herum, besah Stuben und Kammern, wie es Lust hatte,[21] und kam endlich auch an einen alten Turm. Es stieg die enge Wendeltreppe hinauf und gelangte zu einer kleinen Thür. In dem Schlosse steckte ein verrosteter Schlüssel, und als es ihn umdrehte, sprang die Thür auf und saß da[22] in einem kleinen Stübchen eine alte Frau mit einer Spindel und spann emsig ihren Flachs. „Guten Tag, du altes Mütterchen,"[23] sprach die Königstochter, „was machst du da?" „Ich spinne," sagte die Alte und nickte mit dem Kopfe. „Was ist das für ein Ding, das so lustig herumspringt?" sprach das Mädchen, nahm die Spindel und wollte auch spinnen. Kaum hatte es aber die Spindel angerührt, so ging der Zauberspruch in Erfüllung²⁴ und sie stach sich damit in den Finger.

In dem Augenblick aber, wo sie den Stich empfand, fiel sie auf das Bett nieder, das da stand, und lag in einem tiefen Schlafe. Und dieser Schlaf verbreitete sich über das ganze Schloß; der König und die Königin, die eben heimgekommen und in den Saal getreten waren,²⁵ fingen an einzuschlafen und der ganze Hofstaat mit ihnen. Da schliefen auch die Pferde im Stalle, die Hunde im Hofe, die Tauben auf dem Dache, die Fliegen an der Wand, ja, das Feuer,²⁶ das auf dem Herde flackerte, ward still, und schlief ein, und der Braten hörte auf zu brutzeln, und der Koch, der dem Küchenjungen, weil er etwas versehen hatte, an den Haaren ziehen wollte, ließ ihn los und schlief ein. Und der Wind legte sich, und auf den Bäumen vor dem Schlosse regte sich kein Blättchen mehr.

Rings um das Schloß aber begann eine Dornen= hecke zu wachsen, die jedes Jahr höher ward und end= lich das ganze Schloß umzog und darüber hinaus wuchs, daß gar nichts davon zu sehen war, selbst nicht die Fahne auf dem Dache. Es ging²⁷ aber die Sage in dem Lande von dem schönen schlafenden Dornrös= chen, denn so ward die Königstochter genannt, also daß von Zeit zu Zeit²⁸ Königssöhne kamen und durch die Hecke in das Schloß dringen wollten. Es war ihnen aber nicht möglich, denn die Dornen, als hätten sie Hände,[29] hielten fest zusammen, und die Jünglinge blieben darin hängen, konnten sich nicht wieder losmachen und starben eines jämmerlichen Todes.[30] Nach langen, langen Jahren[31] kam wieder einmal ein Königssohn in das Land und hörte, wie ein alter Mann von der Dornenhecke erzählte, es solle[32] ein Schloß dahinter stehen, in welchem eine schöne Königstochter, Dornröschen genannt, schon seit hundert Jahren schliefe, und mit ihr schliefe[33] der König und die Königin und der ganze Hofstaat. Er wußte auch von seinem Großvater, daß schon viele[34] Königssöhne gekommen wären[35] und versucht hätten, durch die Dornenhecke zu bringen, aber sie wären darin hängen geblieben und eines traurigen Todes gestorben. Da sprach der Jüngling: „Ich fürchte mich nicht, ich will hinaus[36] und das schöne Dornröschen sehen." Der gute Alte mochte ihm abraten, wie er wollte,[37] er hörte nicht auf[38] seine Worte.

Nun waren gerade die hundert Jahre verflossen, und der Tag war gekommen, wo Dornröschen wieder erwachen sollte. Als der Königssohn sich der Dornenhecke näherte,[39] waren es lauter schöne Blumen, die thaten sich von selbst auseinander und ließen ihn unbeschädigt hindurch, und hinter ihm thaten sie sich wieder als eine Hecke zusammen. Im Schloßhofe sah er die Pferde und scheckigen Jagdhunde liegen und schlafen, auf dem Dache saßen die Tauben und hatten das Köpfchen unter den Flügel gesteckt. Und als er ins Haus kam, schliefen die Fliegen an der Wand, der Koch in der Küche hielt noch die Hand, als[40] wollte er den Jungen anpacken, und die Magd saß vor dem schwarzen Huhn, das gerupft werden sollte. Da ging er weiter und sah im Saale den ganzen Hofstaat liegen und schlafen, und oben bei dem Throne lag[41] der König und die Königin. Da ging er noch weiter, und Alles war so still, daß man seinen Atem hören konnte, und endlich kam er zu dem Turm und öffnete die Thür zu der kleinen Stube, in welcher Dornrös= chen schlief. Da lag es und war so schön, daß er die Augen nicht abwenden konnte, und er bückte sich und gab ihr einen Kuß. Als er es mit dem Kuß berührt hatte, schlug Dornröschen die Augen auf, erwachte und blickte ihn ganz freundlich an. Da gingen sie zu= sammen hinab, und der König erwachte und die Königin und der ganze Hofstaat, und sahen einander mit großen Augen an. Und die Pferde im Hof stan= den auf und rüttelten sich; die Jagdhunde sprangen und wedelten;[42] die Tauben auf dem Dache zogen das Köpfchen unter'm Flügel hervor, sahen umher und flogen ins Feld; die Fliegen an den Wänden krochen weiter; das Feuer· in der Küche erhob sich, flackerte und kochte das Essen; der Braten fing wieder an zu brutzeln, und der Koch gab dem Jungen eine Ohrfeige, daß er schrie, und die Magd rupfte das Huhn fertig." Und da wurde die Hochzeit des Königssohnes mit dem Dornröschen" in aller Pracht gefeiert, und sie lebten vergnügt bis an ihr Ende.

1. Was für eine Tochter bekamen der König und die Königin? — 2. Beschreiben Sie das Fest, das der König anstellte! — 3. Warum wünschte die dreizehnte weise Frau der Königstochter den Tod? — 4. Auf welche Weise milderte die zwölfte weise Frau den bösen Spruch der dreizehnten? — 5. Erzählen Sie, was an dem Tage geschah, als die Königstochter gerade fünfzehn Jahre alt war. — 6. Was trug sich im Schlosse zu, als die Königstochter den Stich empfand? — 7. Wie lange mußten sie schlafen? — 8. Was geschah während der hundert Jahre? — 9. Warum gab man der Königstochter den Namen Dornröschen? — 10. Hatte es niemand versucht, das schöne Dornröschen zu sehen? — 11. Was erzählte der alte Mann dem Königssohne? — 12. Erzählen Sie, was der Königssohn im Schlosse erlebte!

NOTES.

1.

1. **Friedrich der Große** (1740–1786), *Frederick the Great*, king of Prussia. Masculine and feminine names of persons take no other inflexional ending but -$\mathfrak{s}$ for the genitive, unless they end in -e or a sibilant, when they take -n$\mathfrak{s}$ or -en$\mathfrak{s}$; thus, **Friedrich**, *gen.* **Friedrichs**; **Luise**, *gen.* **Luisens**; **Fritz**, *gen.* **Fritzens**. When the proper name is followed by an adjective, both are declined; thus, *nom.* **Friedrich der Große**, *gen.* **Friedrichs des Großen**, *dat.* **Friedrich dem Großen**, *acc.* **Friedrich den Großen**. In a title the adjective must be written with a capital letter. — **2.** Verbs ending in –ieren always have the accent on the syllable -ier; **inspizier'en, ich inspizier'e, er inspiziert'**. In simple or principal sentences, the verb follows the subject, — *normal* order. — **3. Spandau**, a fortified city, near Berlin; famous penitentiary. — **4. sich erkundigen bei einer Person**, to ask *of a person*, **nach einer Sache**, *after a thing*. — **5. Der Gefangene**, past participle of **fangen**, 'to catch,' here used as a noun. Such nouns are declined like adjectives; thus, *nom.* **der Gefangene**, *gen.* **des Gefangenen**, *dat.* **dem Gefangenen**, *acc.* **den Gefangenen**, *pl.* **die Gefangenen**; **ein Gefangener**, *pl.* **Gefangene**. — **6.** In a sentence introduced by any word, phrase or clause not belonging to the subject, the verb precedes the subject, — *inverted* order. — **7. unschuldig zu sein**, *to be innocent*. Infinitives in German stand at the end of a phrase or clause. — **8. einer** = **ein Gefangener**. When **ein** is used as a pronoun it is declined like the definite article (not like the indefinite article). — **9.** A pronoun object often precedes a noun subject, when the sentence has the inverted order. Note the dative object after **antworten**. — **10.** An interrogative sentence with or without interrogative pronoun has the inverted order. — **11. braven**, pronounce

43

braten (v = w); in German words (usually initial) v is pronounced like f; thus, vier = fier; in foreign words and after vowels it has the sound of w. Final v is always pronounced like f: brav = braf.—
12. hinaus, like most compound adverbs, has the accent on the second compound instead of on the first.

Remarks.—1. Make it a rule to learn every German noun with its article. Never say: Strafe, Anstalt, Verbrechen, but die Strafe, die Anstalt, das Verbrechen, and soon the German gender will become a simple and natural thing.

2. The use of prepositions and cases should receive special attention.

3. "Get into the habit of looking intensely at words, and assuring yourself of their meaning, syllable by syllable, nay, letter by letter. You might read all the books in the British Museum, if you could live long enough, and remain an utterly illiterate, uneducated person; but if you read ten pages of a good book, letter by letter, that is to say with real accuracy, you are forevermore in some measure an educated person." Ruskin.

2.

1. **trägt,** from tragen. Strong verbs with the stem-vowel a are apt to modify this vowel in the second and third person singular of the present indicative; thus, ich trage, du trägst, er trägt. —2. **um den Hals,** *around its neck.* In referring to parts of the body or of clothing the definite article is commonly used in German instead of the English possessive when there can be no doubt as to the possessor. When, however, it seems necessary to point out the possessor, German usually employs the dative (of interest) in this connection; thus, dem Bettler in den Hut, lit. 'to the beggar into the hat,' *into the beggar's hat.*—3. **wirft,** from werfen. Strong verbs (with two exceptions: gehen and stehen) change the radical vowel e (short) into i and e (long) into ie, in the second and third person singular of the present indicative and in the singular of the imperative; thus, ich werfe, du wirfst, er wirft.—4. **Eines Tages,** *one day;* adverbial genitive of (indefinite) time. Compare jeden Tag, above, adverbial accusative of definite time. —5. **vergißt,** from vergessen. Compare note 3.

Note that ﬀ changes into ß, when included in one syllable. —
6. **läuft — nach** (with dative object), from nachlaufen. The adverbial
component (nach) of a compound verb (nachlaufen) is separated from
the verb in all simple tenses and stands at the end of the clause;
thus, er läuft ihm nach. Laufen inflects its present indicative: ich laufe,
du läuffft, er läuft, wir laufen, etc. — 7. **ich nicht**, *not I.*

Remarks. — 1. Carefully note the order of words in each clause.
— 2. Always account for inflexional endings of all nouns and
adjectives.

3.

1. **Barbaroffa** (*red beard*) is the surname of Frederick the First;
emperor of Germany (1152–1190). According to a popular legend
this emperor never died but is sleeping in the Kyffhäuser, a mountain
in Thuringia, until Germany is restored to its former greatness.
—2. **der Musikant'**, *pl.* die Musikanten. Masculine foreign nouns
usually take the ending -en in all cases singular and plural, the
nominative singular alone being without this ending. —3. **darzubringen**, infinitive of the compound verb darbringen. The particle
zu of the infinitive is written in one word between the two components.
—4. **Mitternachtsstunde** (die Mitte, middle + die Nacht, night + die
Stunde, hour), *hour of midnight.* —5. **gehen . . . hinauf**, see hinauf-
gehen. Compare 2, 6. —6. **schlägt**, from schlagen; compare 2, 1. —
7. **die Prinzeffin**, feminine of der Prinz. The word really has two
feminine endings, -eß and -in, which is due to the fact that the Germans
do not feel the foreign ending -eß as a feminine ending. —8. **in der
Hand**, *in her hand;* compare 2, 2. —9. **auf sie zu**, *up to them.* An
adverb is frequently added after a noun or pronoun governed by a
preposition, to define more nearly the relation expressed by the
preposition. Compare the English *from this day on.* —10. **thut sich
auf**, *opens*, from sich aufthun. —11. **ziehen . . . nach**, see nachziehen. —
12. **Effen und Trinken**, *food and drink.* The infinitive is used in
German as noun of the neuter gender. —13. **bietet . . . an**, see anbieten. —14. In dependent clauses the verb stands at the end; this
is called the *transposed* order of words. —15. **brechen . . . auf**, see
aufbrechen. —16. **nicht . . . zu**, see zunicken. —17. **zum** (zu einem) **Au-**

4

denken, *as a keepsake.*—18. aus dem Berge heraus, *outside the mountain.* Compare note 9.—19. werfen ... fort, see fortwerfen. —20. lachen und schelten über, laugh and scold *at.*—21. solch ein, *such a.* Solch preceding the indefinite article is not declined; but ein solches Geschenk.—22. behält, see behalten; compare 2, 1.— 23. nach Hause, *home;* zu Hause, *at home.*—24. giebt, see geben; compare 2, 3.—25. laufen ... zurück, see zurücklaufen.—26. um ... zu suchen, *in order to look for.* The infinitive with um zu expresses design or purpose. The preposition um should always begin the clause, while zu cannot be separated from its infinitive.

Remarks.—1. Analyze all compound words. Compare Mitter= nachtsstunde, note 4. Die Strafe, punishment, die Anstalt, institute, Strafanstalt =? das Geld, money, das Stück, piece, das Geldstück =? die Nacht, night, die Musik, music, die Nachtmusik =? der Mond, moon, der Schein, shine, der Mondschein =? das Auge, eye, der Blick, glance, der Augenblick =? Which word gives the gender to the compound, the first or the last?

2. Carefully distinguish between a compound verb and a simple verb with a prefix. A compound verb consists of two independent words, which under certain conditions must be separated again. A prefix (be=, ge=, er=, ent=, ver=, zer=) is no longer a word and, therefore, cannot stand by itself.

3. Note carefully, here and hereafter, the idiomatic use of pre-positions. Compare notes 20 and 23.

4.

1. ging ... ein, see eingehen.—2. gekommen war, *had come.* In-transitive verbs denoting a change of place or condition form their compound tenses with the auxiliary sein instead of haben; thus, ich bin gekommen, ich war gekommen, ich werde gekommen sein; ich bin eine Wette eingegangen, 'I have accepted a bet.'—3. The suffix =heit forms abstract feminine nouns from nouns and adjectives; hence, die Kind= heit, *childhood,* die Kühnheit, *boldness.*—4. nur (only) is frequently used after an imperative to emphasize the entreaty, just like the English *pray, please, do, just.*—5. ein Schläfchen halten, idiom, *take a nap.* Das Schläfchen is the diminutive of der Schlaf.—6. schlief ...

ein, see einſchlafen. Compare ſchlafen, *to sleep*, with einſchlafen, *to fall asleep*, denoting the transition from the state of waking into that of sleeping; hence, ich habe geſchlafen, but ich bin eingeſchlafen. The same difference exists between wachen and erwachen in the next sentence; thus, ich habe gewacht, but ich bin erwacht.—7. **gegen Sonnenunter=gang**, *toward* or *about sunset*. The preposition gegen (against) often means *about, nearly, almost*. Gegen Mittag =?—8. **zum Laufen**, lit. 'for the running,' *to run*. Note that the article is not omitted in German before abstract nouns (zum = zu dem). Compare 3, 12.—9. **auf=ſprang**, see aufſpringen. In the transposed order of words compound verbs are not separated. In a principal clause we would say, of course, er ſprang eiligſt zum Laufen auf.—10. **rief . . . entgegen**, see entgegenrufen.—11. **vor Müdigkeit**, *from fatigue*. The preposition vor (before) often denotes cause, especially with words expressing emotion. In such phrases the article is always omitted. The suffix =keit is related to =heit (note 3) and forms abstract feminine nouns from adjectives in =er, =el, =en, =ich, =lich, =ſam, and =bar.—12. **wer**, as a relative pronoun, *he who*.—13. This is a German proverb. Find English equivalents.

Remarks.—1. Make it a rule to learn from the beginning the principal parts of all strong verbs.

2. All idiomatic expressions should be memorized, since there is no other way of remembering them.

5.

1. **bei ſtrenger Kälte**, *in severe, cold weather*. The suffix =e added to adjectives forms abstract feminine nouns; thus, kalt, die Kälte; die Strenge =? Bei is the preposition generally used in speaking of the weather; thus, bei kaltem Wetter, *in cold weather*.—2. **Frau Nachbarin**, *Mrs. Neighbor*. In German Herr (Mr.) and Frau (Mrs.) are also used before titles, as a sign of politeness. After Frau the feminine suffix =in is usually omitted in the title. This rule, how-ever, is not strictly observed, especially in colloquial German. The cricket having to ask a favor wishes to treat the ant with a great deal of respect, and therefore, gives her the title of Frau and addresses her in the second person plural (leiht) which was once the

formal pronoun of address instead of Sie. The ant on the other
hand, speaking with the familiarity of a superior, addresses the
cricket with bu.—3. The adversative boch, *nevertheless, yet,* with
a verb in the imperative has the same force as nur. Compare 4, 4.—4. The affirmative adverb ja, *yes,* is often used
within a sentence in the sense of *indeed, you know, why! to be sure,*
etc.—5. bazu, lit. 'there to,' *for it.* The personal pronouns er, fie,
es, referring to things without life, are rarely used, in the dative and
accusative after prepositions, but are replaced by the respective
cases of berfelbe, biefelbe, basfelbe, or by ba (before vowels bar)
with the preposition appended; thus, bazu, *to it,* zu ihm, *to him;*
barin, *in it,* in ihr, *in her.*—6. Frau Grille in conjunction with the
pronoun bu sounds ironical.—7. im Sommer, *in summer;* the
names of the seasons are always preceded by the article in German
(im = in bem).—8. gefungen and mufiziert' are past participles of
fingen and mufizie'ren. Note that verbs in -ieren never take the prefix
ge= of the past participle.—9. Nun, followed by a comma, is an
interjection meaning *well!*—10. fo often introduces a principal
clause preceded by a dependent one, and then need not be translated. It merely resumes the idea expressed in the preceding
dependent clause.

Remark. One of the first difficulties encountered in learning a
foreign language is, that the organs of speech refuse to utter the
foreign sounds easily and fluently. As a piano-player practices a
difficult passage until the fingers play it, so to speak, by themselves,
so should a sentence be repeated over and over again until it can
be spoken fluently. The above fable is readily adapted to conversation between pupils.

6.

1. kraftlos, here an adverb. Note that every adjective may be
used as an adverb, but in that case it remains uninflected. The
suffix =los (English *-less*) means *without;* fchlaflos =? ziellos =?—
2. beren, *whose,* genitive plural of the relative pronoun ber, bie, bas,
which differs from the definite article in the genitive singular of all
three genders (*m.* beffen, *f.* beren, *n.* beffen) and in the genitive and
dative plural (*gen.* beren, *dat.* benen).—3. bisher', *until now.* Com-

pare 1, 12.—4. Note that the verb ſein also forms its compound tenses with the auxiliary ſein, although it does not denote change of place or condition. Compare 4, 2.—5. ſeiner los wurden, *got rid of him.* The adjective los sometimes governs a genitive object.—6. mit ben Hörnern, *with his horns.* Compare 2, 2.—7. ſelbſt preceding the noun it modifies, *even,* following it, *self;* thus, ſelbſt ich, *even I;* ich ſelbſt, *1 myself.*—8. eble for ebele. Adjectives in -er, -el, -en, when inflected, commonly omit the e of these endings.—9. ſtand . . . babei, see babeiſtehen.—10. ſchweigend, present participle of ſchweigen, 'to be silent,' *in silence.*—11. Eins hinter die Ohren geben, idiom, lit. 'give one behind the ears,' *give a box on the ear.* Eins, here used as noun, refers to einen Schlag.—12. halten followed by the preposition für means *to consider, deem.*—13. ſich rächen an (with dative), *to take revenge on.*—14. ſchaden governs an object in the dative case; thus, er ſchadet mir (not mich).

Remark.—1. The rule referred to in note 8 is only an instance of a very important law of euphony, viz. that no two syllables with unaccented e should follow each other. Bearing this law in mind one can see the reason why masculine and neuter nouns in -er, -el, -en, -chen, and -lein take -s (never -es) in the genitive singular, and why they omit the e in the dative singular, and have no ending in the plural. Verbs with a prefix (be-, ge-, er-, ent-, ver-, zer-) never take the prefix ge- of the past participle. Other instances will be cited in the notes when there is occasion for it.

2. In German many intransitive verbs require a genitive or dative object. As this object frequently appears in English as direct object such verbs should receive special attention.

7.

1. The endings -ig and -lich (English -y and -ly) are the most common adjectival suffixes; thus die Eile, *haste,* eilig =? der Hof, court, höflich =?—2. Ancona, a seaport and fortress on the Adriatic Sea in Italy.—3. Bauersleute, plural of Bauersmann. Compounds with Mann take in the plural Leute when no reference is made to sex; hence Bauersleute would include both men and women. Compare Ehemänner, *married men,* with die Eheleute, *married couple,* i. e. husband and wife.— 4. namens (des Namens) *called.* The genitive

case is frequently used in German to denote adverbial relations of time, place, or manner. Compare 2, 4. Many of such genitives are now treated like real adverbs and are, therefore, written with a small initial letter.—5. The conjugation of the modal auxiliaries is defective in English, most of them being used only in the present tense. The missing forms must, therefore, be supplied from other verbs; thus, idṣ muß gehen, *I must go*, idṣ mußte gehen, *I had to go.*—6. von (English *by*) is the preposition used with a verb in the passive.—7. eines Tages, *one day.* Compare 2, 4.—8. des Weges, *that way.* Compare note 4.—9. Barfüßermönch is a monk belonging to the Franciscan or Carmelite Order. Following the example of Christ these monks wore sandals instead of shoes and stockings; hence the name Barfüßermönch, i. e. bare-foot (barfuß) monk.—10. idṣ gehe nicht mit, *I am not going with him.* Mit used adverbially is rendered by *with* accompanied by a pronoun, or by *along.*—11. sprang . . . herbei, see herbeispringen.—12. bot . . . an, see anbieten.—13. zum (zu einem) Wegweiser, *as a guide.* Compare 8, 17.—14. nahm . . . mit, see mitnehmen. Compare note 10. —15. mit Bewilligung, *with the consent.* The suffix -ung (related to English -*ing*) forms feminine nouns from verbs; thus, bewilligen, die Bewilligung; die Verspottung =? die Verachtung =?—16. trat . . . ein, see eintreten.—17. gewannen ihn lieb, *became fond of him.*— 18. Read am vier und zwanzigsten April fünfzehn hundert fünf und achtzig. Note the use of the preposition an with days and times of the day; thus, am vierten April, am Mittag.—19. wurde zum Papste erwählt, *was elected Pope.* Verbs denoting choosing, electing, appointing, are followed by the preposition zu.—20. Read Sixtus der Fünfte. Sixtus V (1585–1590) was the greatest pope of the century. He began life as a shepherd boy. His name was Felix Peretti. He was a powerful ruler, restoring order in Rome, and erecting great buildings (the dome of St. Peter's Church), and founding the Vatican library.

Remarks.—A clear insight into German word-derivation will greatly facilitate the reading; hence the importance of such suffixes as -heit, -keit, -ung, -in, -ig, -lich, -los, etc.

Word Exercise.—verständig =? der Freund =? täglich =? die Schlechtigkeit =? die Aufrichtigkeit =? die Freundlichkeit =? die Blind=

heit =? die Klugheit =? elternlos =? die Demut =? die Unschuld =?
sträflich =? die Wahl =? die Größe =? die Erwartung =? die Ver-
folgung =? die Kränkung =? schädlich =?

8.

1. **Es war einmal,** *once upon a time there was,* a very common
beginning of fairy tales. Einmal, like most compound adverbs, has
the accent on the last word, unless it means 'one time' or 'on one
occasion.' Es is grammatical subject, which is used in German
whenever the logical subject (ein Hirtenknabe) follows the verb and
no adverb commences the sentence.—2. **das,** *who,* here a demonstrative pronoun, not relative, as is shown by the position of the
verb which in a relative clause would have to be at the end. The
use of the demonstrative is quite frequent in German, especially in
the colloquial style.—3. **weit und breit,** *far and wide,* is a common
tautological phrase. German abounds in coupled words, connected
partly by sound, partly by sense.—4. **ließ ... kommen,** lit. 'caused
to come,' *sent for.* Note the causative force of laffen.—5. **Kannst
du** = wenn du kannst, *if you can.* The inverted order frequently
expresses a condition.—6. The use of the present tense in the sense
of the future is much more frequent in German than in English.—
7. Note this colloquial use of the inverted order before direct quota-
tions, and compare the English Mother Goose rhyme: Says the owner,
"Go round, — With your gun and your hound," etc.—8. **viel** may
be fully declined, but is often left uninflected, especially in the
singular.—9. **Tropfen Wasser,** *drops of water.* After nouns signi-
fying measure or weight a noun designating the substance measured is
commonly put in apposition.—10. Compare 5, 2. Herr König, of course,
would not be the proper address. It should be Eure (Ew.) Majestät,
Your Majesty.—11. Note the respectful second person plural (laßt,
Euch) and compare the familiar du used by the king.—12. **am
Himmel,** *in the sky.* Compare im Himmel, *in heaven.*—13. **Bogen
Papier,** *sheet of paper.* See note 9.—14. **zu sehen waren,** *could*
(were to) *be seen.* Note the infinitive active after sein, where the
English would employ an infinitive passive.—15. **gar nicht,** *not at
all.*—16. **einem die Augen,** *one's eyes.* Compare 2, 2. The in-
definite pronoun man, *one,* can be used only in the nominative case,

the missing forms are supplied by the respective cases of ein.—
17. **war dazu imstande,** *was able to do it.*—18. **Hinterpommern,**
Lower Pomerania. **Pommern,** divided by the river Oder into **Hinterpommern** and **Vorpommern,** is a Prussian province on the Baltic Sea.
—19. **De'mant,** more commonly **Diamant'.** Note the difference in
the accent.—20. Compare note 2.—21. **hat eine Stunde in die
Höhe,** idiom, *is one hour in height.* **Stunde** is a very common
measure of distance in Germany, and means the distance one can
walk on foot in an hour. Compare 5, 1.—22. **alle hundert Jahre,**
every hundredth year.—23. **ist vorbei,** *will be past.* Compare note 6.
—24. The prefix **be-** often serves to form transitive verbs from in-
transitives: **antworten, eine Frage beantworten.**—25. **ein Weiser,** *a
wise man,* adjective used as noun. Compare 1, 5.

Remarks. Words with the diminutive endings **-chen** or **-lein** are
neuter. This rule is without a single exception. Compare **der
Bube, das Büblein; die Frau, das Fräulein.**

Word Exercise.—**die Weisheit** =? **königlich** =? **dreimal** =? **ewig** =?
pünktlich =? **der Ruhm** =? **tief** =? **breit** =? **stündlich** =? **Bübchen** =?
—The compounds, **Weltmeer, Schweinehirt, Mittagssonne**—difference
in formation?

9.

1. **allerlei,** *all sorts of.* The suffix **-lei** added to a numeral means
kinds of, sorts of. The numeral preceding this suffix is declined like
an adjective in the feminine gender (genitive), but the compound
is invariable; thus, **viererlei** = 'of four kinds.'—2. **nahm ... ab,** see
abnehmen.—3. **es geht nicht mit rechten Dingen zu,** *things don't go as
they ought to.* This phrase suggests supernatural means, witchcraft.—4. **dem Übel abzuhelfen,** *to remedy the evil.* Note the dative
object.—5. **hieß sie warten,** *asked her to wait.* The modal auxiliaries
and the following verbs **sehen, hören, fühlen, heißen, helfen, lassen,
machen, lehren, lernen** are accompanied by a simple dependent infinitive.—6. **über ein Weilchen,** *after a little while.*—7. **ein Jahr
lang,** *for a year.* **Lang** after expressions of time denotes duration.
Compare the English *all night long, the livelong day.*—8. **in der
Nacht,** *at night,* is an exception to what has been said in 7, 18.—
9. Compare 8, 9.—10. **sich,** dative, *for themselves.*—11. **alle Tage,**

every day; den ganzen Tag, *all day.* Compare 8, 22.—12. Laſſen Sie mir, *let me keep.*—13. noch ein, lit. 'still one,' *another,* i. e. a second one. Compare ein anderes, lit. 'an other' i. e. a different one.—14. es, *there.* Compare 8, 1.—15. nichts als, *nothing but.* —16. Inverted order; why?—17. ſtehn = ſtehen.—18. ſehn (ſehen) auf, *attend to, look to.*

Remark.—The e of the inflexional ending *-en* is silent in colloquial German. Teachers and students, wishing to pronounce distinctly, often overlook that the pronunciation of this e is not at all German. In ordinary colloquial German the ending *-en* is heard only as a quick breath through the nose, the tongue and lips remaining in the position required for the letter preceding this ending (voiced n). In a number of verbs the e is often even omitted in writing: ſtehn, ſehn, gehn; in thun and ſein it has been dropped altogether.

Word Exercise.—das Glück =? das Unglück =? unglücklich =? die Erzählung =? die Fröhlichkeit =? das Siegel =? vertrauen =? der Fleiß =? vertrauensvoll =? fehlerlos =? mittellos =?

10.

1. Kalif, *Caliph,* is a high dignitary in the Orient, next in rank to the Sultan, though many Sultans call themselves Caliph. The word means 'vicar, or representative of Mahomet.'—2. The suffix *-ei* is of foreign origin and always accented.—3. fand ſich, *was found.* The passive voice is much less used in German than in English, and is frequently replaced by a reflexive form, or man with an active verb.—4. ausſchlug, see ausſchlagen.—5. nahm ihr weg, *took away from her;* see wegnehmen. Verbs of taking, stealing, etc., like their opposites, the verbs of giving, presenting, etc., are accompanied by an indirect object, which in English is usually expressed by the preposition *from;* thus, ich gebe ihm das Buch, *I give him the book.* Ich nehme ihm das Buch, *I take the book from him.*—6. mit Gewalt, *by force.*—7. Kadi, Arabian judge.—8. der Wittwe Recht gaben, lit. 'gave the right to the widow,' *decided in favor of the widow.*—9. alſo, *therefore, thus* (never *also*) denotes an inference.— 10. ihm um den Hals, *about its neck.*—11. zu der Zeit, *at the time.*

12. **ihm zu Füßen**, *at his feet*. Note the omission of the definite article in this standing phrase. — 13. **gab . . . zu**, see zugeben. — 14. Compare 9, 5. — 15. **dieß**, frequent for dieſes. — 16. **griff . . . an**, see angreifen. — 17. **mit**, *with him*. Compare 7, 10. — 18. **allein'** (alone), here *however*. — 19. Compare 8, 14. — 20. **ungerechterweiſe**, also ungerechter Weiſe, *unjustly*. Adverbs in weiſe always have the accent on the last word. — 21. **das Erbe**, *the inheritance*, synonym of das Erbteil, *the portion*. Compare der Erbe, *the heir*.

Word Exercise. — ungerechterweiſe offers a good example of the way in which words are derived: recht, *right*, gerecht, *just*, ungerecht, *unjust*, ungerechterweiſe, *unjustly*. Compare wiſſen, *to know*, das Gewiſſen, *conscience*, gewiſſenhaft, *conscientious* (haft = having), die Gewiſſenhaftigkeit =? Herz =? herzhaft =? dreiſt =?

11.

1. **im ſiebenjährigen Kriege**, *in the Seven Years' War*, i. e. the war maintained by Frederick the Great of Prussia against Austria, Russia and France (1756-1763). — 2. **ruſſiſch**, *Russian*. The suffix -iſch (English *-ish*) is used in German to form adjectives of nationality; thus, engliſch, ſpaniſch, amerikaniſch, etc. Note the small initial letter. — 3. Compare 10, 5. — 4. **ſchleppte . . . fort**, see fortſchleppen. — 5. **ſieht . . . aus**, see ausſehen. — 6. **einer**, *one;* compare 1, 8. — 7. **der** (demonstrative), **den** (relative), *he, whom*. — 8. **zeigte auf**, *pointed to*. — 9. **fuhr . . . fort**, see fortfahren. — 10. **da'mit**, *with this*. Whenever da stands for the demonstrative, and not for es, it has the accent. — 11. **dem Soldaten auf die Degenkoppel**, *on the soldier's sword-belt*. — 12. **Bravo**, *Bravo*. Pronounce v = w. Compare 1, 9. — 13. **der Duka'ten**, *the ducat*, a gold coin worth about two dollars. — 14. **legte Fürbitte ein**, *interceded*.

Remarks. — 1. Note the frequent use of the definite article with or without a dative of interest instead of the possessive adjective or possessive case.

2. The gender of nouns, principal parts of strong verbs and uses of prepositions and cases must continue to receive special attention.

Word Exercise. — Composition of ſiebenjährig, Einfall, Degenkoppel, Goldſtück, Schlaukopf, Fürbitte? — Synonyms of Junge, aber, fort,

Schäfer? — männlich =? die Aufstellung =? Rußland =? knabenhaft =? Henceforth these word exercises will be left to the discretion of the teacher.

12.

1. **Wieland,** famous smith of Germanic mythology.—2. **was** is commonly the relative when the antecedent is a neuter adjective.— 3. **Mimung,** name of a famous sword in Germanic mythology; also called *Baldung,* or *Gram.*—4. **auf folgende Weise,** *in the following manner.*—5. **eine Flocke Wolle;** compare 8, 9.—6. **drei Fuß dick,** *three feet thick.* Masculine and neuter nouns expressing weight and measurement are put in the singular instead of the plural.— 7. **Schneide,** syn. **Schärfe.**—8. **schnitt ... durch,** see durchschneiden. —9. **forderte ... auf,** see auffordern.—10. **hau nur zu,** *don't be afraid to strike;* see zuhauen. Compare 4, 4.—11. **aus Leibes-kräften,** lit. 'out of the strength of your body,' *with all your might.* —12. The prepositions **an, auf, in, nach, vor, zu** are frequently preceded by the adverb **bis** to fix a distance, corresponding to the English *as far as, up to, to.*—13. **mir war** (es war mir), lit. 'it was to me', *I felt.*—14. **als wenn** (or als ob), *as if,* is always followed by a verb in the subjunctive mood.—15. **mir am Leibe,** (*on*) *my body.*—16. **heruntergelaufen wäre,** *had run down.* Imperfect subjunctive. See Remark.—17. **schüttel,** or schüttle. Verbs in -en and -eln frequently omit one of the unaccented *e*'s in the first person singular of the present indicative. See 6, Remark 1.—18. **einmal** (like nur, see 4, 4) is frequently used after an imperative to emphasize the entreaty, just like the English *pray, please, do, just.*—19. **ein halber,** *half a;* in German halb always follows the article.—20. **seit diesem Tage,** *from this day on.*

Remark.—The subjunctive has the same form as the indicative, except in the following three cases:

1. The third person is always like the first: ich habe, er habe (hat).

2. All verbs are regular in the subjunctive: ich wolle (will), du schreibest (schreibst), er sehe (sieht).

3. Strong verbs add *e* and modify the stem vowel to form the imperfect subjunctive: ich sah, *subj.* ich sähe.

13.

1. Siegfried, the greatest mythical king of the Germans, the hero of the "Nibelungenlied."—**2. die Niederlande,** *the Netherlands.* Siegfried was born at Xanten on the Lower Rhine.—**3. uralt,** *very ancient.* The prefix **ur=,** always accented, means *original, primitive, very ancient;* hence, der Urwald, *primitive forest,* Ursache, lit. 'original thing,' *cause.*—**4. dessen ganzes Trachten dahin ging,** *whose endeavors all tended to.*—**5. gab . . . nach,** see nachgeben.—**6. bei einem Schmied,** *at a smith's.* The preposition bei often has the meaning *at the house* (*or place*) *of.*—**7.** Compare 9, 5.—**8.** The prefix **zer=** means *to pieces;* zerspringen =? zerbrechen =?—**9.** The imperfect of werden has two forms in the singular: ich wurde (ward), du wurdest (wardst), er wurde (ward), wir wurden, ihr wurdet, sie wurden. Ich ward, etc., are older forms.—**10. fürchtete sich vor,** *was afraid of.* Carefully note all verbs that are reflexive in German but not in English.—**11. sich entledigen,** *to get rid of,* takes an object in the genitive case. Compare 6, 5.—**12. mußte Siegfried vorbei,** supply gehen. The dependent infinitive is often omitted after the modal auxiliaries when it can be easily implied.—**13. werde töten,** *would kill,* subjunctive of indirect discourse. Note that the German employs the tense which would be used in the direct discourse, which in this case would be: dieser wird töten.—**14. fuhr . . . los** (auf), *flew at.*—**15.** The suffix **=nis** (English *-ness*) forms nouns from adjectives; die Wildnis, *wilderness.*—**16.** The prefix **ge=** is added to nouns to form collectives: der Wurm, das Gewürm; der Busch, das Gebüsch =? It is also added to verbs to denote the result or the means of an action, schenken, *to present,* das Geschenk, *the present.* The great mass of these words are neuter.—**17. ohne sich zu besinnen,** *without stopping to think.*—**18. Untiere,** *monsters.* Un= prefixed to adjectives gives them the opposite sense; as a prefix to nouns it frequently gives a bad sense. The prefix un= usually has the accent. **19. zündete . . . an,** see anzünden.—**20. Ungetüm,** synonym of Untier.—**21. unter . . . hervor,** *from under.*—**22. hinein,** *into it.*—**23. überzogen,** see überziehen.

Remarks.—Compound verbs will no longer be pointed out in the notes; it is believed that the students will now be able to find them in the Vocabulary.

2. The use of the reflexive form is much more common in German than in English. Verbs that are reflexive in German but not in English should receive careful attention.

3. When the two components of a compound word form one new idea it can no longer be separated. Compare the English 'house-key,' i. e. key of a house, but a 'buttercup' is the name of a flower. Compare also the English verbs 'to undertake,' 'to overlook,' and the German überzie'hen (over + draw), *to cover.* Such verbs are treated like simple verbs with a prefix.

Suggestive Questions. — Can you give a common-sense reason why the subjunctive is more regular than the indicative?

14.

1. **als guter Sohn,** *as a good son.* After **als** the article is usually omitted. — 2. The prefix **ent=** often means *away from;* entlaufen =? — 3. Note the dative object with aufwarten. — 4. The shorter form **dies** for dieses is quite common especially when no noun follows. — 5. **wenn die Reihe sie traf,** *when it was their turn.* — 6. In conjunction with verbs the adverb **gern,** *gladly, willingly,* is often best rendered by *to like to, to be fond of:* sie übertrugen gern, *they liked to make over.* — 7. **Page** being a foreign noun the **g** is pronounced like *s* in 'pleasure.' — 8. **wollte sich etwas vor= lesen lassen,** *wanted to be read to.* — 9. Here the subjunctive expresses a possibility and might be rendered *whether possibly there were.* — 10. The simple infinitive is often used after finden, but here the present participle is also quite frequent. — 11. **über** with the dative often denotes occupation; thus, er war über denselben einge= schlafen, *he had fallen asleep over it,* i. e. writing it. — 12. In a letter all pronouns of address must be written with a capital. — 13. Compare note 9. — 14. Compare note 10. — 15. **bat er um Vergebung,** *he asked his pardon.* — 16. Compare 7, 19. — 17. **immer höher,** *higher and higher.* Note the force of immer with a comparative. — 18. Note the dative object with dienen.

Suggestive Questions. — Can you give a reason why die Klingel, *bell,* does not add =en to form the infinitive klingeln? Can the verbs unter= stützen and übernehmen be separated?

15.

1. **Rübezahl,** the famous mountain spirit of the Giant Mountains in Silesia. — 2. **sich,** *for himself.* — 3. **bei guter Schlittenbahn,** *when the road is good for sledging.* Compare 5, 1. — 4. **dabei,** *at the same time.* — 5. **recht in Gedanken,** *absorbed in thought.* — 6. **auf ihn zu,** *toward him.* Compare 3, 9. — 7. **was ihm fehle,** *what was the matter with him.* Subjunctive of indirect discourse. — 8. Compare 4, 4. — 9. **ehe sich's der Bauer versah,** *before the peasant was aware of it.* **Es** in **sich's** is not the accusative; it is here, as often, used for **dessen;** compare thus, **ehe er sich dessen versah.** — 10. **bis,** compare 12, 12. 11. **Groschen,** a small silver coin worth about 2¼ cents. Since the year 1871, no longer in circulation. — 12. **gefallen** governs a dative object. — 13. **zum Spielen,** *to play with.* Compare 4, 8. — 14. **darnach,** usual for **danach.** — 15. **so ein** = **solch ein,** *such a.* This use of **so** is common. — 16. **ein paar,** *a few;* compare **das Paar,** *pair.* — 17. This **zu,** *toward,* may be regarded as adverbial component of **zuziehen,** or as postpositive (a preposition following its noun). Note dative object. — 18. **blutarm',** *very poor.* When such compounds as **blutarm** express a high degree, they have the accent on the second word. In its literal sense (= **blut'arm**) this word means *anæmic.* — 19. **eine schöne Zeit,** *a long time.* — 20. **machen** is here, as often, *to give.* Compare **es macht mir Vergnügen,** *it gives me pleasure.* — 21. **am andern Morgen,** *on the next morning.* — 22. **ihm zu Hilfe kommen,** *come to help him.* — 23. **nach Hause;** compare 3, 23.

16.

1. **Segringen,** a little town in Suabia. It is told that when Hebel, a poor theological student, left the university of Tübingen he passed the little town of Segringen (on his way home), where he was taken for a Jewish peddler on account of his shabby clothes. As it was customary in that town to levy a tax upon all Jews, Hebel had to pay it in spite of his remonstrances. The poet revenged himself later on by writing some very amusing little stories about the town: **der Star von Segringen, der Barbier von Segringen.** — 2. Compare 6, 7. — 3. Note the dative case governed by **nützlich.** — 4. Compare the words **Meister,** *master,* and **Geselle,** *journeyman,* in **Siegfried,** which with

Lehrjunge, *apprentice,* form the three grades of a profession.—
5. aufgab, *gave to learn.* Compare die Aufgabe, *exercise.*—6. z. B.,
zum Beispiel, *for example.*—7. So, so, lala, senseless words, meaning
tolerably, fairly well, if used in answer to an inquiry for one's health.
—8. *par Compagnie,* French, pronounce *gnie* like yee and accent the
last syllable.—9. Dolpatsch is a clumsy person. The word is
derived from the Hungarian tolpas, *broad-* or *flat-footed,* a humorous
name given to the Hungarian foot-soldier who appeared slow and
clumsy in comparison with the famous Hungarian cavalry.—
10. titulieren, *to call* (as by a title).—11. er, i. e. der Meister.—
12. In former times the barbers used to be the surgeons of the
town.—13. nach und nach, *gradually.*—14. drein, for darein. This
a is frequently omitted.—15. Compare 13, 14.—16. Hansel,
dialectic diminutive of Hans. The ending =el, corruption of =lein, is
heard all over Germany.—17. The inflexional ending =e is frequently
omitted especially in colloquial German. In some cases it is almost
always omitted, and then the apostrophe may be omitted too; thus
in the singular imperative of lassen; laß for lasse.—18. hier zu Land,
idiom, *here abouts, in this part of the world.*—19. In German the
present tense is frequently used in lively narration.—20. was für
ein, *what kind of a,* inflects only the ein; für has no prepositional
force in this phrase and may also be separated from was.—
21. Compare 9, 8.—22. vor Lachen, *for laughing.*—23. zu Atem
kommen, phrase, *to catch one's breath again.*—24. also, *thus* (never
also), denotes an inference.

17.

1. noch immer, *even now.*—2. eine merkwürdige ... aufgeklärte
Weise. Adjectives with other words depending upon them may be
used as epithets in German, standing immediately before the noun.
This is a characteristic German idiom, which in English should be
rendered by adjective clauses following the noun.—3. kam zu Tode,
phrase, *met its death.*—4. denken an, *to think of.* When a verb
governing a preposition is followed by a dependent infinitive, the
union of the preposition with da must be used; thus, ich dachte daran,
zu gehen, lit. 'thought of it to go,' *I thought of going.*—5. Excursion',

foreign word; hence the accent on the last syllable. — 6. See note 5. 7. Note the dative object with zugeſellen.—8. hatte ſich ihrer bemächtigt, *had taken possession of her.* Note the genitive object ihrer. See 6, Remark 2.—9. kam . . . hervorgeſtürzt, *came rushing out.* Kommen is followed by a past participle in German in the sense of a present participle to express the manner of motion.—10. Subjunctive of indirect discourse.—11. Zumpts Grammatik, Zumpt's Latin Grammar, a famous book, an abridged edition of which (der kleine Zumpt) was used in almost every school.—12. wo, here, as often, *when.*—13. Compare 10, 8.—14. verſchied (syn. ſtarb) an, *died of.*

18.

1. Compare 8, 1.—2. Compare 8, 2.—3. am allerliebſten, lit. 'fondest of all.' A superlative is frequently preceded by aller (genitive plural) for the sake of emphasis; supply hatte ſie.—4. The meaning is that she could never give her enough.—5. The preposition von denotes material.—6. das ſtand ihm wohl, idiom, *that was becoming to her.*—7. Rotkäppchen, lit. 'Little Redcap,' *Little Red Ridinghood.*—8. Compare 8, 9.—9. ſei hübſch artig, *be sure to be good.* In colloquial style hübſch and ſchön are frequently used adverbially in the sense of *very.*—10. ich will ſchon, *I will not fail to.* Schon, 'already,' is often used to emphasize an assurance.—11. wie, is frequently used for als.—12. Note the dative object with begegnen.—13. ſich fürchten vor, to be afraid *of.*—14. Schönen Dank, *thank you very much.*—15. Wo hinaus, lit. 'whither out to,' *where;* supply gehen.—16. ſoll ſich etwas zu gut thun, idiom, *is to have a treat.*—17. Compare 5, 4.—18. bei ſich, *to himself.*—19. ſieh einmal', *just look.* Compare 12, 18.—20. du gehſt ja für dich hin, *why, you just walk straight ahead.*—21. als wie, often for ſo wie, *just as.*—22. Note the genitive case after voll. Compare 6, Remark 2. —23. doch, *still, anyway,* with strong accent.—24. geradeswegs, *straightway.* Compare 7, 4.—25. ohne zu ſprechen, *without speaking.* German always uses an infinitive after prepositions.— 26. machte ſich auf den Weg, idiom, *set out.*—27. es wird mir zu Mut, idiom, *I feel.*—28. that einen Satz, *made a leap.*—29. ob ihr etwas fehlt, *whether anything is the matter with her.*—30. wie war's

fo buntel, *how dark it was.*—31. Note the accent in leben'big.—
32. fich tot fiel, lit. 'fell himself dead,' *fell dead.*

19.

1. Baron von Münchhaufen, *Baron of Münchhausen,* the hero of
most marvelous adventures. The preposition von denotes nobility.
—2. bie Flinte, *shot-gun,* synonyms: bie Büchfe, *rifle,* bas Gewehr,
gun.—3. ganz unb gar, *entirely.* Compare 8, 3.—4. brachte mich
auf ben Einfall, lit. 'brought me upon the idea,' *suggested the idea to
me.*—5. bas Schrot, synonym of ber Hagel.—6. Laffen used
reflexively often expresses the idea of possibility, and then may be
rendered by *can be, may be, fit for, good for,* etc.; thus, fo gut fich's
thun ließ, *as well as it could be done.* Compare bies Waffer läßt fich
nicht trinken, *this water is not fit to drink.*—7. fo wie, *just when.*—
8. fieben Stück, *seven of them.* Note the use of Stück, 'piece,' in this
sense, and compare the English 'I paid two [dollars apiece for them.'
Note also that Stück has the singular form.—9. wie gefagt, i. e. wie
ich gefagt habe, *as I said.*—10. ftieß mir auf, *I met.*—11. Es wäre
Schabe gewefen, *it would have been a pity.* Conditional subjunctive.
Note that the pluperfect subjunctive has the same meaning as the second conditional, es würbe Schabe gewefen fein. The imperfect subjunctive corresponds in meaning to the first conditional; thus, es wäre
Schabe, or es würbe Schabe fein. The conditionals can only be used
in the main clause.—12. Kugel= ober Schrotfchuß = Kugelfchuß ober
Schrotfchuß, *shot with a bullet or small shot.* When several compound
words having the same final member follow one another, it is the
usage in German, to omit the common member except in the
last word, noting the omission in the other cases by a hyphen
appended to the former member.—13. Herr Reinefe is the proper
name of the the fox in German folk-tales and poetry.—14. bafür,
instead of it.—15. larbatfchte, *whipped,* from the Hungarian scourge
or whip of leather.—16. machen wieber gut, *make up for.*—
17. ganz allein, *all alone.*—18. Subjunctive, why?—19. fürbaß,
about, on; obsolete.—20. noch immer, *still;* immer need not be
translated.—21. bas übrig gebliebene Enbchen, *the remaining end.*
—22. fo — fo — boch, *however — yet.*—23. gefaßt auf, *prepared*

5

for. — 24. mit genauer Not, *with great difficulty.* — 25. aus Leibes-
kräften, *with might and main.* — 26. nach mir, *at me.* — 27. dafür,
in return for this. — 28. ganz und gar nicht, *not at all.* Note the
coupled words ganz und gar. — 29. von statten ging, *succeeded.*

Exercises. — Tell these adventures (*a*) in the third person, (*b*) in
indirect discourse.

20.

1. Dornröschen, lit. 'little brier-rose,' *Sleeping Beauty.* — 2. vor
Zeiten, *in days of yore.* — 3. The verb sometimes remains in the
singular with several subjects following. — 4. wenn wir doch ein
Kind hätten, *if we only had a child.* The imperfect subjunctive is
used to express a wish, as unreal or contingent. Such a wish
closely resembles a condition, hence the use of the adverb doch to
emphasize the wish. — 5. bekam, *received* (never *became*). — 6. vor
Freude sich nicht zu lassen wußte, idiom, *could not contain himself for
joy.* — 7. der Verwandte and der Bekannte are declined like adjectives; hence, ein Verwandter, die Verwandten, etc. Compare 1, 5. —
8. The twelve Wise Women remind us of the three Fates of
Northern mythology. Sometimes there appears a thirteenth, which
however is always wicked and inimical to man. — 9. The conjunc-
tions damit, *in order that,* and damit nicht, *lest,* are frequently
followed by a verb in the subjunctive; thus, *in order that they might
be,* etc. — 10. ihrer dreizehn, *thirteen of them.* — 11. zu wünschen ist,
is to (can) be wished. — 12. elf and zwölf, frequently add an e when
they are used without a noun, in that case the f is pronounced like w.
— 13. ihre Sprüche eben gethan hatten, *had just said their say.* —
14. oder nur, *or even.* — 15. gern bewahren wollte vor, *was anxious
to preserve from.* — 16. ließ ausgehen, lit. 'caused to go forth,' *issued.*
— 17. or: sollten verbrannt werden. — 18. an dem Mädchen, *in the person
of the maiden.* — 19. wo, here, as often, *when.* — 20. allerorten (aller
Orten), *everywhere.* — 21. wie es Lust hatte, *as she had a mind to.* —
22. und saß da, supply es before saß, *and there sat.* — 23. du altes
Mütterchen, *you dear old woman,* diminutive of endearment —
24. ging in Erfüllung, *was fulfilled.* — 25. waren is auxiliary to both
heimgekommen and getreten. — 26. ja, das Feuer, *the very fire,* or *even
the fire.* Note the force of ja. — 27. es ging, *was current.* — 28. In

such phrases where the noun is repeated the article is always omitted.—29. **als hätten sie Hände,** for als wenn sie Hände hätten. Als in the sense of als wenn or als ob is followed by the subjunctive and the inverted order.—30. **eines jämmerlichen Todes,** adverbial phrase of manner. Compare 7, 4.—31. **nach langen Jahren,** *many years afterwards.*—32. **solle** and **schliefe,** subjunctives of indirect discourse.—33. Compare note 3.—34. **schon viele,** lit. 'already many,' *many before him.*—35. Subjunctive of indirect discourse.—36. **ich will hinaus,** supply gehen. Compare 13, 12.—37. **der gute Alte . . . wollte,** *however much the good old man dissuaded him.*—38. **er hörte nicht auf,** *he would not listen to.*—39. **näherte sich,** *approached,* with dative object.—40. **als** = als ob. Compare note 29.—41. Verb in the singular. Compare note 3.—42. **wedelten,** supply mit dem Schwanze, *wagged their tails.*—43. **rupfte fertig,** *finished plucking.*—44. The definite article is frequently used colloquially with proper names. It should always be used with proper names when they are preceded by an adjective; thus, das schöne Dornröschen.

TRANSLATION EXERCISES.

1.

1. In Spandau is a large penitentiary. —2. Ask him his name!¹
—3. The prisoner is guilty. —4. He claims to be innocent. —5. One
of the prisoners is innocent. —6. Does he deserve his punishment?—
7. Answer me! —8. What is he doing among them? —9. He is an
honest fellow. —10. Out with him!

¹ der Namen; See note 4.

2.

1. The beggar is standing on the bridge with a large dog. —
2. The placard has an inscription. —3. The young man is compassionate and gives the beggar a coin. —4. Throw the coin into his
hat! —5. Do not forget to give the beggar his coin. —6. Who is
blind? —7. They run after him. —8. She wears a chain¹ about her
neck. —9. Do not run after me! —10. Ask² the beggar about his
dog!

¹ die Kette. —² See 1, note 4.

3.

1. What is the surname¹ of Frederick the First? —2. A merry
musician is walking up the mountain. —3. Do you hear² what the
clock strikes in the village below? —4. Follow me! —5. She
beckons me to follow her. —6. What has he in his hand? —7. Offer
the beggar food and drink! —8. She gives her a present for a keepsake. —9. Do not laugh at the blind beggar! —10. Are you going
home? —11. His wife is not at home. —12. The other musicians do
not keep their gifts.

¹ der Beinamen. —² hören.

4.

1. One day[1] a snail decided to enter into a race with a hare. — 2. The hare made a few leaps, and then laid down under a shady bush to take a nap. — 3 Meanwhile the snail was slowly creeping[2] towards the goal. — 4. Toward sunset the hare sprang up to run the race, but the snail was already at the goal, and laughed at him. — 5. Just see how quickly the hare runs up the mountain! — 6. The snail was very bold to enter into a race with a hare. — 7. He had fallen asleep, when I came. — 8. What did he call out to you? — 9. He had wakened when the door opened.[3] — 10. He has offered her a bet, and she has accepted it.

[1] Comp. 2, 4. — [2] friedjen, frod, getrodjen. — [3] Comp. 3, 10.

5.

1. I loaned him the money. — 2. We started in severe, cold weather. — 3. Was the cricket hungry? — 4. A cricket said to an ant: "Give me some food!" — 5. In summer the ants gather food for the winter. — 6. The ant has no time for singing! — 7. The old beggar had had nothing to eat. — 8. Well, what did he reply to you? — 9. Why, that is foolish! — 10. He who makes music in summer, may dance in winter. — 11. As he had worked in his youth,[2] he had food when he was old. — 12. Do go home quickly!

[1] Comp. 4, 8. — [2] bie Jugenb.

6.

1. I have had a sleepless night. — 2. A lion was dying in front of his lair. — 3. When the malicious fox saw the dying lion, he taunted him. — 4. Formerly the lion had persecuted the animals, and now they were glad to get rid of him. — 5. Even the lazy donkey vented his hatred on the dying lion. — 6. Only the horse did not avenge himself on his enemy, although the lion had injured him most. — 7. Do not take revenge on an enemy who can no longer harm you! — 8. Do be silent! — 9. He gave him a box on the ear. — 10. Oxen have horns, and wild boars have tusks. — 11. I pity you. — 12. I consider him a mean fellow.

7.

1. Felix was the son of poor peasants in Italy—2. Although he was very poor and had to herd swine, he was always courteous and obliging.—3. One day, when the weather was very bad, a monk passed[1] through the village and asked for a guide.—4. None of the other boys were willing to show him the way to his cloister.—5. When Felix had politely greeted the monk, he went with him.—6. The monk soon found[2] that the boy had a good mind.—7. The parents gave their consent, and the monk took the boy with him to the monastery.—8. Felix remained there and studied so diligently that he soon became very learned.—9. As he was always modest and courteous, everybody became fond of him.—10. He soon became [a][3] cardinal, and finally was elected pope.

[1] kommen. —[2] erkennen. —[3] Words in [ ] are not to be translated.

8.

1. It was known far and wide that the shepherd boy could answer all questions.—2. Even[1] the king had heard of it and had sent for the boy.—3. The king proposed three questions to the boy.—4. If the boy can answer the king's questions the king will treat him as his own child.—5. It is impossible to answer the questions which the king proposed to the boy.—6. The boy showed the king that his questions could not be answered.—7. When the king asked: "How many stars are [there] in the sky?" the boy took a sheet of paper and made so many dots on it that the king was unable to count them.—8. Then the boy said: "[There][2] are as many stars in the sky as [there are] dots on this paper. If you do not believe me, just count them."—9. What is here to be seen?—10. Every hundredth year Frederick Barbarossa awoke from his sleep.

[1] Comp. 6, 7. —[2] Omit, or translate by es.

9.

1. Once upon a time there was a woman who had all sorts of misfortunes.—2. One day she went to a hermit who lived in the near-by forest and told him of her misfortune.—3. "Wait a moment,"

said the hermit, then he went out and after a while returned with a little box. — 4. The box was sealed, and the hermit told the woman to carry it about in her house three times a day. — 5. The woman did as the hermit had told[1] her, for she put great confidence in the remedy. — 6. One evening as she was carrying the box about, she saw that the maids were baking a cake for themselves in the kitchen. — 7. Every day she had to remedy an evil. — 8. She kept the box for a year and then took it back to the hermit. — 9. The hermit would not let her have the box another year, but he gave her the remedy which it contained. — 10. The box contained nothing but a paper with an inscription.

[1] ḥelfen.

10.

1. The poor woman refused the caliph's offer. — 2. She did not want to sell her property, because she had inherited it from her forefathers. — 3. When the overseer of the royal gardens took the land away from her by force, the poor widow went to the judge. — 4. The laws of the land decided in favor of the poor woman, but the caliph was accustomed to consider his wishes as the highest law. — 5. One day, when the caliph was on the property which his overseer had taken from the poor woman, he saw the judge riding into the garden. — 6. The judge carried a sack and was riding on a donkey. — 7. When the judge saw the caliph, he threw himself at his feet and asked him to help him fill the sack with earth. — 8. But they could not lift the sack upon the donkey. — 9. Now the judge said: "If you find this burden too heavy, how will you be able to carry the poor widow's inheritance?" — 10. The caliph returned to the widow all the land which the overseer had taken away from her.

11.

1. A shepherd boy was tending his sheep in a meadow. — 2. A Russian soldier robbed him of one of his sheep. — 3. As the soldier would not return the sheep to him, the boy secretly made a red line on his sword-belt. — 4. Then he went to the colonel of the Russian

regiment and asked him to punish the soldier. — 5. When the regiment was standing in line[1] the boy easily recognized the soldier who had stolen his sheep. — 6. "How did you find the thief?" asked the colonel of the boy. — 7. The boy pointed to the red line on the soldier's sword-belt, and said: "I marked him with this piece of red chalk in order to recognize him." — 8. "That was a good idea," said the colonel and gave the boy a ducat. — 9. When the colonel wished to punish the soldier, the boy interceded for him. — 10. What does the shepherd boy do with the red chalk? He marks his sheep with it.

[1] angetreten war.

12.

1. Once upon a time there was a very famous smith, called Wieland. — 2. Wieland entered into a competition with Amilias, the armorer of king Neidung. — 3. Amilias had forged a suit of armor, and Wieland was to make a sword. — 4. Mimung was the most famous sword in the world. — 5. After Wieland had tested the sword, he went to the court of king Neidung. — 6. Amilias laughed at Wieland and asked him to strike with all his might. — 7. Wieland did not strike, but placed the edge of his sword on Amilias' helmet and pressed a little. — 8. When Wieland pressed a little harder, his sword cut through Amilias' suit of armor. — 9. Amilias scarcely felt it, when Wieland's sword passed through his body. — 10. But when he moved, he fell down dead![1]

[1] tot hinfallen.

13.

1. Siegmund, king of the Netherlands, had a son, called Siegfried. — 2. When Siegfried was a boy, he asked his father to let him go abroad. — 3. Siegmund thought that his son was too young to seek adventures. — 4. When his father finally consented, Siegfried entered the service of a smith who lived in a forest. — 5. Siegfried swung the hammer so powerfully that the anvil broke in pieces. — 6. The smith was afraid of the young hero and wished to get rid of him. — 7. One day when Siegfried had to go through the forest a dragon attacked him. — 8. Siegfried killed the dragon and then

bathed[1] himself in its blood.[2]—9. Between the shoulders was the
only spot where Siegfried was vulnerable.—10. Another legend
tells us that a linden leaf[3] had fallen between his shoulders as he
was bathing in the dragon's blood.

[1] ſich baben. —[2] das Blut. —[3] das Lindenblatt.

14.

1. Have you heard of the page who became [an] officer on
account of his filial love?—2. Frederick the Great made him an
officer.—3. As the boy could not support his mother from his salary
he mounted guard for others.—4. When the king could not sleep
at night, the page had to read to him.—5. Once the poor boy had
fallen asleep when the king called him.—6. The king read the
letter which the page had written to his mother.—7. He was
pleased with the noble heart of the youth.—8. I thank you.—9. I
beg your pardon.—10. Now it is his turn.

15.

1. On a cold winter day a poor peasant went into the forest to
fetch some wood.—2. In the forest he saw a man with a sledge.—
3. The man asked him whether he could help him.—4. Rübezahl
helped him load the wood upon the sledge, and went home with the
peasant.—5. The peasant gave him food and drink, and also some
money.—6. Rübezahl was pleased with the poor peasant, who
gladly gave as much as he could.—7. The peasants[1] had two
pretty children, a boy and a girl.—8. Rübezahl called the children
to him, and gave each a present.—9. When he had gone away, the
peasants found that the bullets, which Rübezahl had given to the
children, were of pure gold.—10. Then they were very happy and
thanked the good mountain-spirit,[2] who had made them rich.

[1] Comp. 7, 3.—[2] der Berggeiſt.

16.

1. A fowler once caught many birds in his net.—2. He took
them out one after another, twisted their necks and threw them on
the ground.—3. But he was frightened when one of the prisoners

cried: "I am the barber of Segringen." — 4. It was the barber's starling, which had learned to speak. — 5. The barber's apprentice had taught him to speak. — 6. The starling had joined a company of other birds, which unfortunately flew into the fowler's net. — 7. When the fowler took the bird back to his master, he received a good reward. — 8. When it became known how clever the bird was, everybody wished to hear it speak. — 9. People laughed when the starling called the apprentice a blockhead. — 10. The starling had heard his master call the apprentice a blockhead, when he broke a medicine bottle.

17.

1. I once had a white mouse that was so tame that it ran about among the books which lay on my desk. — 2. One day we caught a wild mouse and we put it in the cage with the tame one. — 3. But the wild mouse gnawed a hole through the wooden box and disappeared. — 4. Since that time the white mouse was very restless and often tried to jump from the table. — 5. Finally it followed the wild mouse. — 6. After some time we heard a terrible noise and the white mouse came rushing out of the mousehole. — 7. The wild mice had bitten it and its coat was covered with blood. — 8. When we had given it some milk we laid it on cotton. — 9. But the poor little mouse died of its wounds. — 10. My sister maintained that it had died of a broken heart.

18.

1. Once upon a time there was a little girl who was called Red Ridinghood, because she always wore a red hood. — 2. One day Red Ridinghood's mother had baked some cakes; then she asked her little daughter to take some to her sick grandmother. — 3. On the way to her grandmother's house Red Ridinghood met a wolf. — 4. "Why don't you pick some flowers for your grandmother?" said the wolf. — 5. While Red Ridinghood was picking flowers in the forest, the wolf ran to her grandmother's house and devoured the old woman. — 6. Then the wolf put on her cap, lay [down] in her bed and drew the curtains. — 7. The wolf jumped out of the bed and devoured the little girl. — 8. A hunter who was passing the house

heard the snoring, and when he entered the room, he saw the wolf lying in the bed. — 9. Soon he saw a red hood, and the little girl jumped out of the wolf. — 10. Also the old grandmother was still alive and thanked the hunter who had saved them.

19.

1. Baron of Münchhausen was a hunter who is famed far and wide for[1] his remarkable adventures. — 2. In a Russian forest he once met a black fox. — 3. As he did not wish to riddle its fur with shot, he loaded his gun with a large nail. — 4. Then he fired and was so fortunate [as] to nail the fox's tail to a tree. — 5. With his hunting-knife he made a cross-cut on the fox's face and then whipped him out of his skin. — 6. Another time when he was trying a new shotgun, he was attacked by a wild boar. — 7. In great haste the Baron jumped behind a large tree. — 8. The boar pierced[2] the tree with its tusks. — 9. As the boar could not pull its tusks out of the tree, the baron was saved. — 10. Then he bound the boar with ropes and took it home alive.

[1] wegen. — [2] fahren burch.

20.

1. On her fifteenth birthday[1] Dornröschen was alone in the castle. — 2. As she was walking about in the castle she came to a little room in the tower. — 3. Here she saw an old woman who was busily spinning. — 4. Dornröschen had never seen a spindle and she asked the old woman to show her one. — 5. But when she touched it, she pricked herself and fell asleep. — 6. The hedge grew higher and higher.[2] — 7. "Behind this hedge is a castle," said the old man, "and in it a beautiful princess has been sleeping for a hundred years." — 8. The youth was not afraid and wanted to penetrate the hedge. — 9. When the youth kissed Dornröschen, she awoke from her sleep. — 10. After the wedding the prince took Dornröschen with him to his father's castle.

[1] ber Geburtstag. — [2] Comp. 14, 17.

VOCABULARY.

Explanations. — To each noun is added the gender and the nominative plural (if the noun has a plural); thus, Abend, *m.*, -*e*, meaning that Abend is a masculine noun having in the plural the ending *-e*; Bant, *f.*, (feminine gender), *ᴬe* (plural: Bänte). A dash (—) indicates the repetition of the title-word.

The ending of the genitive singular has been given when the noun does not follow the general rules for the formation of the genitive case; thus, Bett, *n.*, *gen.* -*eš*, *pl.* -*en*, bed.

The principal parts of strong verbs are given in parentheses; thus geben (gab, gegeben), to give. Separable compound verbs are indicated by a hyphen (-); thus, ab-brüden. The principal parts of the verbal component are given in parentheses; thus, ab-helfen (half, geholfen), meaning abhelfen, half ab, abgeholfen. Verbs having fein as auxiliary are marked by an asterisk (*).

The accent is only indicated when the word does not follow the general rules of accentuation.

Since most German adjectives can be used in their simple form as adverbs, only the adjective is given in English. It must be remembered, however, that for example feierlich also means *solemnly*, though the Vocabulary gives only *solemn*.

The case governed by prepositions, verbs and adjectives is given in parentheses.

A

ab, off, away.

ab-brüden, to fire.

Abend, *m.*, -*e*, evening.

abends, in the evening.

Abenteuer, *n.*, —, adventure.

aber, but, however.

abergläubisch, superstitious.

abgewetzt, see abwetzen.

ab-helfen (half, geholfen), to remedy.

ab-laufen (lief, gelaufen), to run out.

ab-nehmen (nahm, genommen), to diminish.

ab-raten (riet, geraten), to dissuade.

Abschied, *m.*, leave, departure.

ab-stellen, to correct.

ab-wenden (wandte, gewandt), to turn away.

Abwesenheit, *f.*, absence.

73

ab=wetzen, to whet away.

ab=ziehen (zog, gezogen), to sharpen by strapping.

Ach! oh!

ahnen, to suspect.

alle, all.

allein', alone; however.

allerlei, all sorts of.

allerliebst', most of all.

alles, everything.

allmäh'lich, gradually.

als, as, when; as if; than; als ob (wenn), as if; nichts als, nothing but.

also, thus, therefore.

alt, old; die Alte, the old woman.

Alter, n., age.

am = an dem.

Amboß, m., Ambosse, anvil.

Ameise, f., –n, ant.

Amilias, proper name.

an (dat. or acc.), of, in, by, on, from, at.

an=bieten (bot, geboten), to offer.

an=blicken, to look at.

Anco'na, name of a town in Italy.

Andenken, n., —, keepsake.

ander, next, other.

anders, different.

Anerbietung, f., –en, offer.

Anfang, m., "e, beginning.

anfangen (fing, gefangen), to begin, commence.

anfänglich, at first.

an=fassen, to take hold of.

an=greifen (griff, gegriffen), to take hold of.

Angriff, m., –e, attack.

Angst, f., "e, anxiety, fear.

ängstlich, anxious, eager.

an=halten (hielt, gehalten), to urge.

an=kommen* (kam, gekommen), to arrive.

Ankunft, f., "e, arrival.

an=langen,* to arrive.

an=legen, to erect; to take aim with.

an=packen, to take hold of, seize.

an=rühren, to touch.

ans = an das.

ansah, see ansehen.

an=schaffen, to procure, buy.

an=sehen (sah, gesehen), to look at.

ansehnlich, large.

anstatt' (gen.), instead of.

an=stellen, to prepare.

an=thun (that, gethan), to put on.

an=treffen (traf, getroffen), to meet.

an=treten* (trat, getreten), to fall in.

Antwort, f., –en, answer.

antworten (dat.), to answer.

an=zünden, to light, put on fire.

April', April.

arbeiten, to work.

arg, gross, wicked, bad.

arglistig, deceitful.

arm, poor.

artig, neat.

Arznei'glas, n., "er, medicine bottle.

aß, aßen, see essen.

Atem, *m.*, breath.

atmen, to breathe.

auch, also, too.

auf (*dat.* or *acc.*), on, upon.

auf-brechen* (brach, gebrochen), to start, go away.

auf-fliegen* (flog, geflogen), to fly up, alight.

auf-fordern, to challenge, ask.

auf-geben (gab, gegeben), to give to learn.

auf-gehen* (ging, gegangen), to go up, fly up, rise.

aufgeklärt, see aufklären.

aufgestellt, see aufstellen.

auf-heben (hob, gehoben), to preserve, keep; to annul, do away with.

auf-hören, to stop.

auf-klären, to explain.

auf-laden (lud, geladen), to load, pack.

auf-machen, to open.

aufrichtig, candid, honest.

aufs = auf das.

auf-schlagen (schlug, geschlagen), to pitch, raise, open.

auf-schneiden (schnitt, geschnitten), to cut open.

Aufseher, *m.*, —, overseer.

auf-setzen, to put on.

auf-springen* (sprang, gesprungen), to rise, spring open, jump up.

auf-stehen* (stand, gestanden), to get up, stand upon.

auf-steigen*(stieg,gestiegen),to rise.

auf-stellen, to draw up.

aufstieg, see aufsteigen.

auf-stoßen* (stieß, gestoßen), to meet with.

auf-tragen (trug, getragen), to serve up.

auf-thun (that, gethan), *refl.* to open.

auf-wachen,* to wake up.

auf-warten (*dat.*), to wait upon.

Auge, *n.*, *gen.* -s, *pl.* -n, eye.

Augenblick, *m.*, -e, moment.

augenblicklich, instantly.

aus (*dat.*), out of.

aus-dehnen, to extend.

ausdrücklich, explicit.

auseinan'der-thun (that, gethan), to open, separate.

aus-gehen* (ging, gegangen), to go out.

aus-halten (hielt, gehalten), to endure, stand.

aus-lassen (ließ, gelassen), to vent.

aus-richten, to perform, attend to.

aus-schlafen (schlief, geschlafen), to sleep enough (out).

aus-schlagen (schlug, geschlagen), to refuse.

aus-sehen (sah, gesehen), to look.

aus-stehen (stand, gestanden), to endure.

aus-stoßen (stieß, gestoßen),to utter.

aus-strecken (nach), to stretch out for.

aus-streichen (strich, gestrichen), to efface, cross out.

äußerst, extremely.

B

Bache, f., -n, wild sow.

Backe, f., -n, cheek.

backen (buk, gebacken), to bake.

bald, soon.

Bank, f., ᵉe, bench.

Barbaros'ſa, Barbarossa (red beard).

Barbier', m., -e, barber.

Barfüßermönch, m., -e, Franciscan brother.

Baron', m., -e, baron.

bat, see bitten.

Bauch, m., ᵉe, stomach, belly.

Bauer, m., -n, peasant.

Bauersmann, m., -leute, peasant.

Baum, m., ᵉe, tree.

beantworten, to answer.

bedauern, to pity.

bedenklich, critical, serious.

befand, see befinden.

Befehl, m., -e, command, order.

befiel, see befallen.

befinden (befand, befunden), refl., to be.

begab, see begeben.

begangen, see begehen.

begann, see beginnen.

begeben (begab, begeben), refl., to go, betake oneself.

begehen (beging, begangen), to commit.

begehren, to desire.

beginnen (begann, begonnen), to begin

begleiten, to accompany.

begraben (begrub, begraben), to bury.

befallen (befiel, befallen), to befall, seize.

behalten (behielt, behalten), to keep.

behaupten, to maintain, affirm.

beherzt, brave, courageous.

behutſam, careful.

bei (dat.), by, near, in, at, to, with, on.

beide, both, two.

beim = bei dem.

Bein, n., -e, leg, bone.

beina'he, almost.

beiſam'men, together.

Beiſpiel, n., -e, example.

beißen (biß, gebiſſen), to bite.

beißend, sarcastic.

bekam, see bekommen.

Bekannte, m., -n, acquaintance.

bekommen (bekam, bekommen), to receive, get.

belebt, crowded.

bemächtigen, refl. (gen.), to take possession of.

bemerken, to notice, observe.

benachbart, neighboring.

Bettler, m., —, beggar.

bequem, convenient, easy.

bereit'willig, willing, glad.

Berg, m., -e, mountain.

bergab', downhill.

berühmt, famous, celebrated.

berühren, to touch.

beſaß, see beſehen.

beſchämen, to put to shame.

beſchenken, to present, give a present to, reward.

beſchließen (beſchloß, beſchloſſen), to decide.

beſchloſſen, see beſchließen.

beſchneiden (beſchnitt, beſchnitten), to cut.

beſchreiben (beſchrieb, beſchrieben), to describe.

beſchwerlich, troublesome.

beſehen (beſah, beſehen), to look at.

beſinnen (beſann, beſonnen), *refl.*, to reflect.

Beſinnen, *n.*, reflection.

beſonders, especially.

beſſer, better.

beſt, best.

beſtändig, constantly, always.

beſtehen (beſtand, beſtanden) Abenteuer, to encounter adventures.

Beſtie, *f.*, –n, beast.

beſtrafen, to punish.

beſtreichen (beſtrich, beſtrichen), to besmear, rub.

beſtrich, see beſtreichen.

betrachten (*refl.*), to regard, watch, look at.

betrauern, to mourn.

betroffen, taken aback, startled.

betrübt, sad.

Bett, *n.*, *gen.* –es, *pl.* –en, bed.

bewahren (vor), to preserve from.

bewegen, to induce, move.

Bewegung, *f.*, –en, motion.

Bewilligung, *f.*, consent.

bewundern, to admire.

Bier, *n.*, –e, beer.

6

bis (*dat.*), until, till, up to.

Bischen, *n.*, —, a bit, a little.

bisher', until now.

Biſſen, *m.*, —, bite.

Biß, *m.*, Biſſe, bite.

bitten (bat, gebeten), to ask, beg.

blaſen (blies, geblaſen), to blow.

Blatt, *n.*, ⁺er, leaf.

Blättchen, *n.*, —, little leaf.

blau, blue.

bleiben* (blieb, geblieben), to remain, stay.

blicken, to look.

blieb, see bleiben.

blies, see blaſen.

blind, blind.

Blitz, *m.*, –e, lightning.

blos, only.

Blume, *f.*, –n, flower.

blutarm', very poor.

Blutfleck, *m.*, –e, blood-stain.

Boden, *m.*, ⁺, ground.

Bogen, *m.*, —, sheet.

Börſe, *f.*, –n, purse.

böſe, wicked.

bot — an, see anbieten.

brach, see brechen.

brachte, see bringen.

Braten, *m.*, —, roast.

brav, good, honest.

Bravo, bravo!

brauchen, to need.

brechen (brach, gebrochen), to break.

breit, broad, wide.

Breite, *f.*, breadth, width.

brennen (brannte, gebrannt), to burn.

Brief, *m.*, -e, letter.

bringen (brachte, gebracht), to bring, take to.

bringen — zurück, see zurück= bringen.

Bruder, *m.*, ˣ, brother.

Brücke, *f.*, -n, bridge.

brutzeln, to sputter.

Büblein, *n.*, —, little boy, lad

Buch, *n.*, ˣer, book.

Büchse, *f.*, -n, gun, rifle.

bücken, *refl.*, to stoop.

buckelig, hump-backed.

Bürde, *f.*, -n, burden.

Busch, *m.*, ˣe, twig, bush.

D

da, as, since; there; then.

dabei', by, near it; at the same time.

dabei'=stehen (stand, gestanden), to stand by.

Dach, *n.*, ˣer, roof.

dachte, see denken.

dadurch', by it, through it.

dafür', for it, in return for it.

daheim', at home.

daher', therefore.

dahin', thither.

dahin'ter, behind it.

damit', with it; in order that; da'mit, with this.

Dank, *m.*, thanks.

dankbar, thankful.

Dankbarkeit, *f.*, thankfulness.

danken (*dat.*), to thank.

dann, then.

daran', at it, by it.

daran'=geben (gab, gegeben), to give up.

darauf', on it; da'rauf, there-upon.

daraus', out of it.

dar=bringen (brachte, gebracht), to bring, offer.

darin', in it.

darnach', for it, at it, after it.

darü'ber, over it.

darum, therefore.

das, the; this, that; who, which.

da=sein* (war, gewesen), to be there (here).

dastand, see dastehen.

da=stehen (stand, gestanden), to stand there (here).

daß, that.

davon', of it; da'von, of this.

dazu', to it, for it.

Decke, *f.*, -n, cover.

Degenkoppel, *f.*, -n, sword-belt.

dehnen, stretch.

Demantberg, *m.*, -e, mountain of adamant.

demütig, humble.

denken (dachte, gedacht) an, to think of.

Denkmal, *n.*, ˣer, monument.

denn, then; for.

dennoch, nevertheless, for all that.

der, die, das, the; the one; who, which.

deren, *gen.*, whose.

dergestalt, in such a way.

derſelbe, dieſelbe, daſſelbe, the same.

deshalb, therefore.

deſſen, *gen.* of der, whose.

deswegen, therefore, on account of it.

dicht, close.

dick, thick.

die, the; the one; who, which.

Dieb, *m.*, -e, thief.

dienen, serve.

Dienſtfehler, *m.*, —, misdemeanor.

dienſtfertig, obliging.

dieſer, dieſe, dieſes, this, the latter.

Ding, *n.*, -e, thing.

dir, *dat.* of du, you, to you.

doch, yet, pray, anyway, nevertheless.

Dolpatſch, *m.*, -e, blockhead.

Dorf, *n.*, "er, village.

Dorfknabe, *m.*, -n, village boy.

Dorn, *m.*, *gen.* -s, *pl.* -en, thorn.

Dornenhecke, *f.*, -n, thornhedge.

Dornröschen, *n.*, —, Brier-rose, Rosamond (name of the Sleeping Beauty).

dort, there.

Drache(n), *m.*, —, dragon.

Drahtgitter, *n.*, —, wire screen.

draußen, out, outside, out of doors.

drei, three.

dreimal, three times.

drein (darein), into it.

Dreiſtigkeit, *f.*, boldness.

dreizehn, thirteen.

dreizehnt, thirteenth.

drehen, to turn.

bringen (brang, gebrungen), to penetrate.

dritt, third.

drücken, to press.

drum, see darum.

du, you (thou).

Dukaten, *m.*, —, ducat.

dumm, stupid.

dunkel, dark.

durch (*acc.*), through.

durchgeſchnitten, see durchſchneiden.

durchlöch'ern, to riddle.

durch=ſchneiden (ſchnitt, geſchnitten), to cut through.

durchwan'dern, to walk through.

E

eben, just then, just.

edel, noble.

Edelknabe, *m.*, -n, page.

ehe, before.

Ehrenſtelle, *f.*, -n, post of honor, dignity.

ei! oh! why!

Eichbaum, *m.*, "e, oak tree.

eigen, own.

Eigenſinn, *m.*, stubbornness.

Eigentümer, *m.*, —, owner.

Eile, *f.*, haste.

eiligſt, very hastily.

ein, eine, ein, a, an; one.

einan'der, each other, one another.

ein=büßen, to lose.

Einer, one.

Einfall, m., ⁿe, idea.

ein=fallen (fiel, gefallen), to occur.

ein=flößen, to give to drink.

eingebüßt, see einbüßen.

ein=gehen (ging, gegangen), to enter into, accept.

eingeladen, see einladen.

einige, some.

ein=laden (lud, geladen), to invite.

ein=legen, to lay in, put in.

einmal (or einmal'), once, once upon a time, some time, noch einmal, once more.

eins, one.

ein=schlafen* (schlief, geschlafen), to fall asleep.

Einsiedler, m., —, hermit.

einst, once.

einstimmig, unanimous.

ein=treten* (trat, getreten), to enter.

Eis, n., ice.

Eisen, n., iron.

elend, miserable.

elf, eleven.

Eltern, pl., parents.

empfand, see empfinden.

empfangen (empfing, empfangen), to receive.

empfinden (empfand, empfunden), to feel.

emfig, busy.

Endchen, n., —, little end.

Ende, n., gen. -s, pl. -en, end; am Ende, finally.

endlich, at last, finally.

enge, narrow.

entbehren, to do without, miss.

entdecken, to discover.

Entfernung, f., -en, distance

entge'gen=rufen (rief, gerufen), to call out to.

entgegnen, to reply.

enthalten (enthielt, enthalten), to contain.

entledigen, refl. (gen.), to get rid of.

entschließen (entschloß, entschlossen), refl., to resolve.

entsetzlich, terrible.

entstand, see entstehen.

entstehen (entstand, entstanden), to arise.

entweder — oder, either — or.

entzückt über, delighted at.

er, he.

erbauen, to build.

Erbe, n., inheritance.

Erbteil, n., -e, inheritance.

Erde, f., earth.

erfüllen, to fulfil.

Erfüllung, f., fulfilment.

ergreifen (ergriff, ergriffen), to take hold of, seize.

ergriff, see ergreifen.

erhalten (erhielt, erhalten), to receive.

erheben (erhob, erhoben), to exalt, raise; refl., to raise oneself, rise; begin to burn

erhielt, see erhalten.

erhob, erhoben, see erheben.

erholen, *refl.*, to recover.
erinnern an, to remind of.
erkalten,* to become cold.
erkannte, see erkennen.
erkennen (erkannte, erkannt), to perceive, recognize.
erkundigen, *refl.*, (nach), to ask, enquire.
erlauben, to permit, allow.
erleben, to experience.
ernannte, see ernennen.
ernennen (ernannte, ernannt), to appoint.
erreichen, to reach.
errichten, to erect.
erschallen, to sound, resound.
erschlagen (erschlug, erschlagen), to kill.
erschlug, see erschlagen.
erscholl, see erschallen.
erschöpft, exhausted.
erschrak, see erschrecken.
erschrecken (erschrak, erschrocken), to be alarmed, frightened; to frighten.
erschrocken, frightened.
erst, first, only.
erstaunen, to astonish.
erstaunt, astonished.
erwachen,* to awake.
erwählen, to chose, elect.
erwarb, see erwerben.
erwarten, to await.
erweitern, to enlarge.
erwerben (erwarb, erworben), to earn, acquire.
erwidern, to reply.

erzählen, to tell, relate.
es, it.
Esel, *m.*, —, donkey, ass.
Essen, *n.*, —, food, dinner.
essen (aß, gegessen), to eat.
etwas, something, anything.
euch, you.
ewig, eternal, everlasting.
Ewigkeit, *f.*, eternity.
Exkursion, *f.*, –en, excursion.

F

Fabel, *f.*, –n, fable.
Fahne, *f.*, –n, flag.
fahren* (fuhr, gefahren), to ride, drive.
fährt, see fahren.
Fall, *m.*, ˮe, case.
fallen* (fiel, gefallen), to fall.
faltig, wrinkled.
Fami'lienzwistigkeit, *f.*, –en, family quarrel.
fand, see finden.
Fang, *m.*, ˮe, catch.
fangen (fing, gefangen), to catch.
Fanggeld, *n.*, –er, reward.
fast, almost, nearly.
Feder, *f.*, –n, pen.
fegen, to sweep.
fehlen (*dat.*), to miss, lack, be wanting, ail.
Fehler, *m.*, —, fault, mistake.
feierlich, solemn.
fein, fine, delicate.
Feind, *m.*, –e, enemy.
Feld, *n.*, –er, field.

Felix, Christian name meaning "happy."

Fenster, n., —, window.

fertig, ready, finished.

Fest, n., -e, feast, festival.

fest, fast, firm.

fett, fat.

Feuer, n., —, fire.

feuern, to fire.

fiel, see fallen.

finden (fand, gefunden), to find.

fing an, see anfangen.

Finger, m., —, finger.

Flachs, m., flax.

flackern, to flicker.

Flamme, f., -n, flame.

Flasche, f., -n, flask, bottle.

Fleiß, m., industry, diligence.

fleißig, diligent.

Fliege, f., -n, fly.

fliegen* (flog, geflogen), to fly.

fließen* (floß, geflossen), to flow.

Flinte, f., -n, shotgun.

Flocke, f., -n, flock.

flog, flogen, see fliegen.

floß, see fließen.

Flucht, f., flight.

Flug, m., flight.

Flügel, n., —, wing.

flugs, quickly.

Fluß, m., "sse, river.

Flut, f., -en, tide, flood.

folgen (dat.), to follow.

fort, gone, away, off.

fortan', henceforth.

fort-fahren* (fuhr, gefahren), to continue.

fort-kommen* (kam, gekommen), to get along.

fort-schleppen, to drag away.

fort-springen* (sprang, gesprungen), to spring away.

fort-werfen (warf, geworfen), to throw away.

Frage, f., -n, question.

fragen, to ask.

Frau, f., -en, wife, woman, Mrs.

freigesprochen, see freisprechen.

freilich, to be sure.

frei-sprechen (sprach, gesprochen), to acquit.

freiwillig, voluntary, from free will.

Fremde, f., foreign country; in die —, abroad.

fressen (fraß, gefressen), to eat, devour.

Freude, f., -n, joy, enjoyment, pleasure.

freuen, refl. (über), to be glad of, rejoice.

Freund, m., -e, friend.

freundlich, friendly.

Friede(n), m., peace.

friedlich, peaceful.

Friedrich, Frederick.

frisch, fresh.

Frischling, m., -e, young wild boar.

froh, glad.

fröhlich, joyful.

fromm, pious.

früh, soon, early.

früher, formerly.

frühzeitig, early.

Fuchs, m., ˣe, fox.

fühlen, to feel.

fuhren, see fahren.

führen, to conduct, guide.

Führer, m., —, guide.

fuhr fort, see fortfahren.

füllen, to fill.

fünfzehn, fifteen.

fünfzehnt, fifteenth.

für (acc.), for.

fürbaß, about, on.

Fürbitte, f., -n, intercession; — einlegen, to intercede.

fürlieb nehmen, to put up with, be content with.

furchtbar, terrible.

fürchten, refl. (vor), to be afraid of.

fürchterlich, terrible.

Fürst, m., -en, sovereign, monarch.

Fuß, m., ˣe, foot.

Fußboden, m., ˣ, floor.

G

gab, gaben, see geben.

gab nach, see nachgeben.

Gabe, f., -n, gift.

gähnen, to yawn.

ganz, quite, all, whole, entire; — und gar, entirely, — und gar nicht, not at all.

gar, very; — nicht, not at all.

Garn, n., -e, net.

Garten, m., ˣ, garden.

Gast, m., ˣe, guest.

gebacken, see backen.

Gebäude, n., —, edifice, building.

geben (gab, gegeben), to give; es giebt, there is, there are.

Gebirge, n., —, mountains.

geblieben, see bleiben.

gebracht, see bringen.

Gebrauch, m., ˣ, use.

gebrauchen, to use.

gebräuchlich, customary.

gebrechlich, frail, feeble.

gebrochen, see brechen.

Gedanke, m., -n, thought.

gediegen, pure, solid.

gedulden, refl., to have patience.

geduldig, patient.

gefährlich, dangerous.

gefallen (gefiel, gefallen), to please (dat.).

gefällig, obliging, kind.

gefangen, see fangen.

Gefangene, m., -n, prisoner.

gefaßt (auf), prepared for.

gefielen, see gefallen.

gefressen, see fressen.

gefunden, see finden.

gegen (acc.), against, toward, about.

Gehalt, m., ˣer, salary.

gehen* (ging, gegangen), to go.

geht zu, see zugehen.

geizig, covetous, avaricious.

gekommen, see kommen.

gelangen* (zu), to arrive at, attain; get, come.

gelaufen, see laufen.

Geld, n., –er, money.
Geldſtück, n., –e, coin.
Gelegenheit, f., –en, lay of the land.
gelehrt, learned.
geliebt, beloved.
Gelüſten, n., desire.
Gemüt, n., –er, soul.
genannt, see nennen.
genau, exact.
General', m., ˮe, general.
genommen, see nehmen.
Gequietſch, n., squealing.
gerade, just, straight.
geradeswegs, straightway.
geradezu, straight.
Gerappel, n., rattling.
geraten* (geriet, geraten), to come unexpectedly, happen to come.
geräumig, spacious.
gerecht, just.
Gerechtigkeit, f., justice.
Gerichtstag, m., –e, judgment day.
geriet, see geraten.
gern, gladly; — haben, to like, love.
gerührt (über), moved at.
Geſchäft, n., –e, business.
geſchah, see geſchehen.
geſchehen* (geſchah, geſchehen), to happen.
Geſchenk, n., –e, present.
Geſchmeide, n., —, jewelry.
geſchnitten, see ſchneiden.
Geſchöpf, n., –e, creature.

geſchrieben, see ſchreiben.
geſchwind, quick.
geſchwungen, see ſchwingen.
Geſelle, m., –n, fellow, journey-man.
Geſellſchaft, f., –en, company, party.
Geſetz, n., –e, law.
Geſicht, n., –er, face.
Geſpräch, n., –e, conversation.
geſtern, yesterday.
geſtorben, see ſterben.
geſungen, see ſingen.
gethan, see thun.
getragen, see tragen.
getreten, see treten.
getrieben, see treiben.
getroſt, without fear, confident.
gewachſen, see wachſen.
gewahren, to notice.
Gewalt, f., –en, force, power, might.
gewaltig, mighty.
gewannen lieb, see lieb gewinnen.
Gewehr, n., –e, gun.
geweſen, see ſein.
Gewiſſenhaftigkeit, f., conscien-ciousness.
gewiß, sure, certain.
gewogen (dat.), well disposed.
gewöhnlich, usual.
gewohnt, accustomed.
geworden, see werden.
Gewürm, n., –e, vermin, reptiles.
gezogen, see ziehen.
giebt, see geben.
giftig, poisonous, venomous.

ging, see gehen.
glänzend, shining.
Glas, n., ⁗er, glass.
glatt, smooth.
glauben, to believe,
gleich, like; at once, immediately.
gleichfalls, likewise, also.
gleichwohl', nevertheless.
gleiten* (glitt, geglitten), to glide, drift.
Glied, n., -er, limb.
Glocke, f., -n, clock.
Glück, n., luck, fortune.
glücklich, lucky, fortunate, happy.
Glut, f., heat.
Gold, n., gold.
golden, golden.
Goldstück, n., -e, goldpiece.
Gott, m., ⁗er, god.
Grab, n., ⁗er, grave.
Gramma'tik, f., -en, grammar.
Graukopf, m., ⁗e, gray-headed fellow.
grauen, to dawn.
grausam, cruel.
greifen (griff, gegriffen) nach, to take hold of, seize.
Greis, m., -e, old man.
greulich, horrible.
griff, see greifen.
Grille, f., -n, cricket.
grob, rough, coarse, rude.
Grobheit, f., -en, rudeness.
Groschen, m., —, a German coin.
groß, great; large, tall.
Großmutter, f., ⁗er, grandmother.
Großvater, m., ⁗, grandfather.

grün, green.
grüßen, to greet.
Gürtel, m., —, belt.
gucken, to look.
Gut, n., ⁗er, possession.
gut, good, well; — thun, refl., to give oneself a treat.

H

Haar, n., -e, hair.
Habe, f., possession.
haben (hatte, gehabt), to have.
Hafer, m., oats.
Hagel, m., shot.
haha! oh oh! haha!
Hakkam, proper name.
halb, half.
Hals, m., ⁗e, neck.
halten (hielt, gehalten), to hold; refl., keep; — für, regard, consider, deem.
Hammer, m., ⁗, hammer.
Hand, f., ⁗e, hand.
hangen (hing, gehangen), to hang.
Hansel, dim. of Hans, John.
hart, hard.
Hase, m., -n, hare.
Hast, f., haste.
Haß, m., hatred.
hatte, see haben.
Haube, f., -n, cap.
Hauer, m., —, tusk.
Haufen, m., —, pile, heap.
Haus, m., ⁗er, house, home.
Häuschen, hut, little house.
Hausfrau, f., -en, housewife.

haus=halten (hielt, gehalten), to keep house, live.

Haushaltung, f., —en, household.

heben (hob, gehoben), to lift.

Hecke, f., —n, hedge.

Heil, n., welfare.

heim=kommen* (kam, gekommen), to come home.

heimlich, secret.

Heimweg, m., way home.

heiß, hot.

Held, m., —en, hero.

Helm, m., —e, helmet.

heißen (hieß, geheißen), to be called; to bid, ask.

helfen (half, geholfen), to help.

hell, bright.

her, hither, along.

herab', down.

herab'=gehen* (ging, gegangen), go down stairs.

heran'=kommen (kam, gekommen), to approach, come up.

heraus', out.

heraus'=finden (fand, gefunden), to find out.

heraus'=geben (gab, gegeben), to give back.

heraus'=kommen* (kam, gekommen), to come out.

heraus'=nehmen (nahm, genommen), to take out.

heraus'=springen* (sprang, gesprungen), to jump out.

heraus'=stehen (stand, gestanden), to project.

heraus'=werfen (warf, geworfen), to throw out, eject.

heraus'=ziehen (zog, gezogen), to pull out, draw out.

herbei'=holen, to fetch up.

herbei'=schleichen* (schlich, geschlichen), to move, creep up stealthily.

herbei'=springen* (sprang, gesprungen), to run up.

Herd, m., —e, hearth.

Herde, f., —en, herd.

herein', in.

herein'=treten* (trat, getreten), to step in.

hernach', afterwards.

Herr, m., gen. —n; pl. —en, gentleman, master, sir, Mr.

her'=traben, to trot along.

herum', about, around.

herum'=gehen* (ging, gegangen), to walk about.

herum'=laufen* (lief, gelaufen), to run about.

herum'=springen* (sprang, gesprungen), to jump about, run around.

herun'ter=laufen* (lief, gelaufen), to run down.

herun'ter=sinken* (sank, gesunken), to sink down.

hervor', forth, forward.

hervor'=fließen* (floß, geflossen), to flow forth.

hervor'=kommen* (kam, gekommen), to come forth.

hervor'=stürzen,* to rush out.

hervor'=ziehen (zog, gezogen), to draw out.

Herz, n., gen. -ens, pl. -en, heart.

Herzhaftigkeit, f., courage, manliness.

Heu, n., hay.

heute, to-day.

Hieb, m., -e, cut, thrust, blow.

hielt, see halten.

hier, here.

hiermit, herewith, enclosed.

hieß, see heißen.

Hilfe, f., help; zu — kommen, to come to his help.

hilft, see helfen.

Himmel, m., sky, heavens.

hin, thither; — und her, to and fro.

hinauf=gehen* (ging, gegangen), to go up.

hinauf=steigen* (stieg, gestiegen), to climb up.

hinaus', out.

hinaus'=bringen (brachte, gebracht), to take out.

hinaus'=eilen,* to hasten out.

hinaus'=schauen, to look out.

hindurch', through.

hinein', in, into.

hinein'=fahren* (fuhr, gefahren), to penetrate.

hinein'gethan, see hineinthun.

hinein'=tauchen, to dip in.

hinein'=thun (that, gethan), to put in.

hinein=treten* (trat, getreten), to step in.

hindurch'=fahren* (fuhr, gefahren), to pass through

hin=fallen* (fiel, gefallen), to fall down.

hing, see hangen.

hinten, adv., behind.

hinter (dat. or acc.), behind.

Hinterpommern, n., Lower Pomerania.

hinun'ter, down.

Hirtenbüblein, n., —, shepherd boy.

hoch, high.

Hochzeit, f., -en, wedding.

Hof, m., ˝e, court, courtyard.

hoffen, to hope.

Hoffnung, f., -en, hope.

höflich, polite, courteous.

Höflichkeit, f., politeness.

Hofstaat, m., court, courtiers.

Höhe, f., -n, height.

höher, higher.

Höhle, f., -n, cave, den.

höhnen, to jeer, sneer.

hold (dat.), kind.

holen, to fetch, get.

Holz, n., wood.

Holzkasten, m., ˝, wooden box.

Holzstoß, m., ˝e, wood-pile.

hören auf, to hear; to listen to.

Horizont', m., -e, horizon.

Horn, n., -e or ˝er, horn.

Hornhaut, f., ˝e, horny skin.

Hornschicht, f., -en, horn-layer.

Hosentasche, f., -n, trousers' pocket.

hübsch, pretty.

Huf, *m.*, –e, hoof.

Huhn, *n.*, ˣer, fowl, chicken, partridge.

hülflos, helpless.

Hund, *m.*, –e, dog.

Hündchen, *n.*, —, little dog.

hundert, hundred.

hundertjährig, lasting for a hundred years.

Hunger, *m.*, hunger.

hüpfen, to hop, dance.

husch, quick.

husten, to cough.

Hut, *m.*, ˣe, hat.

hüten, to herd, tend.

J

Ibn Beschir, proper name.

ich, I.

ihm, to him.

ihn, him.

ihnen, them, to them.

Ihnen, to you.

ihr, her, their; to her.

im = in dem or einem.

immer, always, ever.

imstan'de, able.

in (*dat.* or *acc.*), in.

indem', while.

indes', meanwhile.

Inschrift, *f.*, –en, inscription.

inspizie'ren, to inspect, examine.

inständig, urgent.

Ita'lien, *n.*, Italy.

ja, yes; yea; indeed, why!

Jagd, *f.*, –en, hunt, hunting.

Jagdgeschichte, *f.*, –en, hunting story.

Jagdhund, *m.*, –e, hound, hunting dog.

Jäger, *m.*, —, hunter.

Jahr, *n.*, –e, year.

jährlich, yearly.

jämmerlich, pitiful, miserable.

jammern, to lament.

je, ever.

jeder, jede, jedes, every, everybody.

jedermann, everybody.

jedoch', however.

jemals, ever.

jemand, somebody, anybody.

jetzt, now.

Jubel, *m.*, rejoicing.

Jugend, *f.*, youth.

jung, young.

Junge, *m.*, –n, boy, lad.

Jüngling, *m.*, –e, youth.

K

Kadi, *m.*, –s, = Richter, judge.

Kaiser, *m.*, —, emperor.

kaiserlich, imperial, royal.

Käfig, *m.*, –e, cage.

Kalif', *m.*, –en, calif.

Kälte, *f.*, cold.

kam, see kommen.

Kammer, *f.*, –n, chamber.

kann, kannst, see können.

Käppchen, n., little hood.

karbat'schen, to whip.

Kardinal', m., -e, cardinal.

Karren, m., —, cart.

Kästchen, n., —, box.

kauen, to chew.

kaufen, to buy.

kaum, scarcely, hardly.

Keiler, m., —, wild boar (two years old).

kein, -e, no, not any.

Keller, m., —, cellar.

Kerl, m., -e, fellow.

Kette, f., -n, chain.

keuchen, to pant.

Kind, n., -er, child.

Kindheit, f., childhood.

kindlich, childlike, filial.

klagen (über), to complain of.

Kleid, n., -er, dress.

klein, small, little.

Klinge, f., -n, blade.

klingeln, to ring the bell.

klingen, to ring.

Klinke, f., -n, latch.

klopfen, to knock.

Kloster, n., ", cloister.

klug, clever, intelligent.

Klugheit, f., cleverness, prudence.

Knabe, m., -n, boy.

Koch, m., "e, cook.

kochen, to cook.

Köhler, m., —, charcoal man.

kommen* (kam, gekommen), to come, get to.

König, m., -e, king.

Königin, f., -nen, queen.

königlich, royal.

Königreich, n., -e, kingdom

Königssohn, m., "e, king's son, prince.

Königstochter, f., ", princess.

können (konnte, gekonnt, pres. ich kann), to be able, can.

konnte, see können.

Kopf, m., "e, head.

Köpfchen, n., —, little head.

kostbar, costly, precious

kosten, to cost.

Kot, m., dirt, mud.

Kraft, f., "e, strength, power.

kraftlos, strengthless.

krank, sick.

kränken, to offend.

Kreuzschnitt, m., -e, cross cut.

kriechen* (kroch, gekrochen), to creep.

Krieg, m., -e, war.

kriegen, to get.

Kröte, f., -n, toad.

Krug, m., "e, mug.

Küche, f., -n, kitchen.

Kuchen, m., —, cake.

Küchenjunge, m., -n, kitchen boy.

Kugel, f., -n, ball, bullet.

Kügelchen, n., —, little ball.

Kugelschuß, m., "e, shot with a bullet.

Kuh, f., "e, cow.

Kühnheit, f., boldness.

kunstfertig, skillful.

kunſtvoll, artistic.
kümmerlich, needy, wretched.
kurz, short, quick.
Kuß, m., ᵘe, kiss.

L

laben, to refresh.
lachen, to laugh (über, at).
laden (lud, geladen), to load.
Ladeſtock, m., ᵘe, ramrod.
lag, see liegen.
Land, n., ᵘer, land, country.
Ländereien, pl., lands.
lang, long; lange, adv., long, for a long time.
langſam, slow.
Lärm, m., noise.
las, see leſen.
laſſen, (ließ, gelaſſen), to let, leave; cause, make.
Lauf, m., ᵘe, barrel.
laufen* (lief gelaufen), to run.
laut, loud, aloud.
lauten, to sound, read; wie lauten, what are.
lauter, nothing but.
Leben, n., life.
leben, to live.
leben'dig, alive.
Lebensjahr, n., -e, year (of life).
lebhaft, lively.
Lebtag, m., live-long.
lecken, to lick.
ledig, empty.
legen, to lay; refl., to lay down, subside.

lehren, to teach.
Lehrjunge, m., -n, apprentice.
Leib, m., -er, body, stomach.
Leibeskraft, f., ᵘe, strength of one's body.
leicht, light, easy.
Leid, n., gen. -es, pl. -en, harm.
leihen, (lieh, geliehen), to lend.
leiſe, gentle.
leiten, to lead, conduct.
Leiter, m., —, guide.
Leitzaum, m., ᵘe, bridle, rein.
lernen, to learn.
leſen (las, geleſen), to read, gather.
letzt, last.
leuchten, to shine, gleam.
Leute, pl., people, men.
Licht, n., -er, light, candle.
lieb, dear, fond; lieb gewinnen, to become fond of; lieb haben, to love.
Liebe, f., love.
lieben, to love.
lieber, rather.
lieblich, lovely.
lief, liefen, see laufen.
liegen (lag, gelegen), to lie.
ließ, see laſſen.
loben, to praise.
Loch, n., ᵘer, hole.
los, loose; los werden, to get rid of.
los=fahren* (fuhr, gefahren) auf, to attack, be down upon one.
los=hämmern (auf), to hammer in upon.

los=kommen* (kam, gekommen), to get loose.

los=laſſen (ließ, gelaſſen), to let loose, set on, release.

los=machen, to loosen, free.

Löwe, m., –n, lion.

lub, see laben.

Luft, f., ²e, air.

Lunte, f., –n, tail.

Luſt, f., ²e, pleasure, desire.

luſtig, merry, joyful.

M

machen, to make, do

Macht, f., ²e, might.

Mädchen, n., —, girl.

Magd, f., ²e, maid servant.

magſt, see mögen.

Mal, n., –e, time.

man, one.

manch, many a.

manchmal, sometimes.

Mann, m., ²er, man, husband.

Maſſe, f., –n, matter.

matt, faint.

Mauer, f., –n, wall.

Maul, n., ²er, mouth.

Maus, f., ²e, mouse.

Manſeloch, n., ²er, mouse-hole.

Meer, n., sea, ocean.

mehr, more; nicht mehr, no longer.

mehrere, several.

mehrfach, several times.

mein, my.

meiſt, most.

Meiſter, m., —, master.

Menge, f., –n, quantity multitude, great many.

Menſch, m., –en man (human being).

merkwürdig, peculiar, remarkable, wonderful.

mich, me.

Milch, f., milk.

mildern, to alleviate. mitigate.

Mimung, proper name.

Minu'te, f., –n, minute.

mir, to me.

miſchen, refl. to mingle.

mit, (dat.), with.

mit=bringen (brachte, gebracht), to bring with one.

mit=gehen* (ging, gegangen), to go with one (along).

mitleibig, compassionate.

mit=nehmen (nahm, genommen), to take with one (along).

Mittag, m., –e, noon.

Mittagsſonne, f., midday sun.

Mittel, n., —, means.

mitten, in the middle; mitten in, in the midst of.

Mitternachtsſtunde, f., hour of midnight.

möchte, see mögen.

mögen (mochte, gemocht), pres. ich mag, to like.

möglich, possible.

Mönch, m., ²e, monk.

Mond, m., –e, moon.

Mondenſchein, m., moonshine.

Moral', f., moral.

mörderiſch, murderous.

Morgen, m., —, morning.

Müdigkeit, f., fatigue, weariness.

Mühe, f., -n, trouble, difficulty.

Mühle, f., -n, mill.

mühsam, with difficulty.

Münchhausen, proper name.

munter, lively, merry.

Musik, f., music.

Musikant', m., -en, musician.

musizie'ren, to make music.

müssen (mußte, gemußt, pres. ich muß), must, to have to.

mußte, see müssen.

Mut, m., courage, mood; zu Mut werden (sein), to feel.

Mutter, f., ⸗, mother.

Mütterchen, n., —, little mother, old woman.

n

nach (dat.), after, to; nach mir, at me; nach und nach, gradually.

nach=ahmen, (dat.), to imitate.

nach=laufen (lief, gelaufen), to run after (dat.).

Nachbarin, f., -nen, neighbor.

Nachbarschaft, f., neighborhood.

nachdem', after.

nach=geben (gab, gegeben), to yield (dat.).

nachher', afterwards.

Nachmittag, m., -e, afternoon.

nach=sehen (sah, gesehen), to inquire, see.

nächst, nearest, next.

Nacht, f., ⸗e, night.

Nachtmusik, f., serenade.

nach=ziehen, (zog, gezogen), to follow.

Nagel, m., ⸗, nail.

nageln, to nail.

nagen, to gnaw.

nah, near, close.

näher, closer.

nähern, refl. (dat.), to approach.

nahm, nahmen, see nehmen.

nahm ab, see abnehmen.

nahm mit, see mitnehmen.

nähren, refl., to support.

Name(n), m., —, name.

namens, called, by the name of.

nämlich, namely, that is.

natür'lich, naturally, of course.

Nebenzimmer, n., —, next room.

nehmen (nahm, genommen), take; with dat., to take away from.

Neidung, proper name.

nein, no.

nennen (nannte, genannt), to call, name.

neu, new.

neugierig, curious.

nicht, not.

nichts, nothing.

nicken, to nod.

nie, never.

nieder=fallen* (fiel, gefallen), to fall down.

Niederlande, pl., the Netherlands.

nieder=lassen (ließ, gelassen), refl., to sit down, settle.

nieder=sinken* (sank, gesunken), to sink down.

niederträch'tig, mean, low.
niemand, noone, nobody.
nimmt, see nehmen.
noch, nor, still, yet; noch ein, another; noch nicht, not yet.
Not, f., need, distress.
nun, now, well!
nur, only, just.
Nußhecke, f., –n, hedge of nut trees.
nützlich, useful.

O

o! o! oh!
ob, whether; als ob, as if.
oben, above.
ober, upper.
Oberst, m, –en, colonel.
obgleich', although.
obschon', although.
Ochse, m., –n, ox.
oder, or.
Ofen, m., ͛, stove.
offen, open.
offenbar, evidently.
Offizier', m., –e, officer.
öffnen, open.
oft, often.
ohne, without.
Ohr, n., gen., –s, –en, ear.
Ohrfeige, f., –n, box on the ear.
Orden, m., –, order.
ordentlich, proper, orderly, well.
Ordnung, f., order.
Ort, m.. –e or ͛er, place.

7

P

paar (par), few.
packen, to pack, seize, grasp.
Page, m., –n, page.
Palast', m., ͛e, palace.
Panzer, m., –, coat of mail, armor.
Papier', n., –e, paper.
Papst, m., pope.
Paul, Paul.
Peitsche, f., –n, whip.
Pelz, m., –e, hide, fur.
Pfeife, f., –n, pipe.
Pferd, n., –e, horse.
pflegen, to care for, take care of,
Pflicht, f., –en, duty.
plagen, refl., to plague, torment oneself.
Platz, m., ͛e, place, spot.
plötzlich, suddenly.
Pracht, f., splendor, magnificence.
preußisch, Prussian.
Prinz, m., –en, prince.
Probe, f., –n, test, trial.
probie'ren, to try.
Protest', m., –e, protest.
prüfen, to try, test.
Punkt, m., –e, point dot.
Pünktlein, n., –, little dot.

R

Rachen, m., –, mouth, jaw.
rächen, refl. (an), to revenge oneself on, take revenge on.

Rand, *m.*, ⁻er, edge.
Rat, *m.*, advise.
rauben, to rob.
rauschen, to rustle.
Recht, *n.*, -e, right.
recht, right, well, regular.
Rede, *f.*, -n, words, language.
Redensart, *f.*, -en, expression, phrase.
regen, *refl.*, to move.
regie'ren, to reign.
Regiment', *n.*, -er, regiment.
Reich, *n.*, -e, empire, kingdom.
reichen, to give, hand.
reichlich, richly, in abundance.
Reichtum, *m.*, ⁻er, wealth, riches.
Reihe, *f.*, -n, turn, row.
Reihenfolge, *f.*, -n, order, succession.
Reinefe, Renard.
reißen (riß, gerissen), to tear.
reiten* (ritt, geritten), to ride.
retten, to save, rescue.
Rettung, *f.*, -en, safety.
richten, to direct.
Richter, *m.*, —, judge.
richtig, right, to be sure.
rief, see rufen; rief entgegen, see entgegenrufen.
rings, round about (in a circle).
riß, see reißen.
ritt, see reiten.
Ritter, *m.*, —, knight.
Rolle, *f.*, -n, roll.
rosig, rosy, pink.
rot, red.
Rötel, *m.*, red chalk.

Rotkäppchen, Little Red Riding hood.
Rübezahl, proper name.
Rücken, *m.*, —, back.
rufen (rief, gerufen), to call, cry.
ruhen, to rest.
ruhig, quiet.
Ruhm, *m.*, fame, glory.
rühren, to move.
rupfen, to pluck (the feathers).
russisch, Russian.
Rüstung, *f.*, -en, armor.
Rußland, *n.*, Russia.
rütteln, *refl.*, to shake oneself.

S

Saal, *m.*, Säle, hall.
Sache, *f.*, -n, thing.
Sack, *m.*, ⁻e, sack.
Sage, *f.*, -n, legend.
sagen, to say.
sah, see sehen.
sammeln, to gather.
Sammet, *m.*, velvet.
Sammetfell, *n.*, -e, velvety coat.
sämmtlich, all.
sanft, gentle.
saß, saßen, see sitzen.
säße, see sitzen.
satteln, to saddle.
Satz, *m.*, ⁻e, leap.
Schachtel, *f.*, -n, box.
Schade(n), *m.*, ⁻, pity, harm.
schaden (*dat.*), to hurt, harm.
Schaf, *n.*, -e, sheep.

Schäferjunge, *m.*, –n, shepherd boy.

schaffen (schuf, geschaffen), to create, make; to bring, take, carry, transport.

schämen über, *refl.*, to be ashamed of.

scharf, sharp.

Schärfe, *f.*, –n, sharp edge.

schattig, shady.

Schatz, *m.*, ˣe, treasure,

scheckig, mottled.

scheinen (schien, geschienen), shine; seem.

schelten, to scold (über, at).

schenken, to present, give.

Schere, *f.*, –n, scissors.

Schermesser, *n.*, –, razor.

schicken, to send; *refl.*, to fit, suit.

schieben (schob, geschoben), to shove, push.

schien, see scheinen.

schießen (schoß, geschossen), to shoot.

Schimpfwort, *n.*, ˣer, insult, invection.

Schlaf, *m.*, sleep.

Schläfchen, *n.*, –, nap.

schlafen (schlief, geschlafen), to sleep.

Schlafgemach, *n.*, ˣer, sleeping room.

Schlag, *m.*, ˣe, blow.

schlagen (schlug, geschlagen), to beat, strike.

Schlaukopf, *m.*, ˣe, cunning fellow,

schlecht, bad.

schleppen, to drag; schleppte fort, see fortschleppen.

schleudern, to fling.

schlief, see schlafen; schlief ein, see einschlafen.

schlimm, bad.

Schlinge, *f.*, –n, snare.

Schlittschuh, *m.*, –e, skate; — laufen, to skate.

Schlitten, *m.*, —, sleigh, sledge.

Schloß, *n.*, ˣer, castle; lock.

Schloßhof, *m.*, ˣe, courtyard.

schlug, see schlagen.

schlüpfen, to slip.

Schlüssel, *m.*, —, key.

schmelzen (schmolz, geschmolzen), to melt.

Schmied, *m.*, –e, smith.

schmieden, to forge.

schmuck, sleek, pretty.

schmunzeln, to smile.

Schnabel, *m.*, ˣ, beak, bill.

Schnäblein, *n.*, —, little beak.

schnarchen, to snore.

Schnäuzchen, *n.*, —, little mouth.

Schnecke, *f.*, –n, snail.

Schnee, *m.*, snow.

Schneebahn, *f.*, –en, sledging.

Schneide, *f.*, –n, edge.

schnell, fast, quick.

Schnitt, *m.*, –e, cut.

schnüffeln, to sniff, smell.

schon, already, surely.

schön, beautiful, handsome.

Schönheit, *f.*, –en, beauty.

Schoß, *m.*, ˣe, lap.

schoß, see schießen.

Schrecken, *m.*, —, terror.

schrecklich, terrible.

schreiben (schrieb, geschrieben), to write.

Schreibtisch, m., -e, desk, writing table.

schreien (schrie, geschrieen), to cry.

schrie, see schreien.

Schrot, n., shot.

Schrotschuß, m., ꞏe, shot with small shot.

schuf, see schaffen.

Schule, f., -n, school.

Schulter, f., -n, shoulder.

Schürze, f., -n, apron.

schütteln, refl., to shake oneself.

schwach, weak.

schwanken, to rock, swing.

Schwanz, m., ꞏe, tail.

Schwänzlein, n., —, little tail.

schwarz, black.

Schweif, m., -e, tail.

schweigen (schwieg, geschwiegen), to be silent.

Schwein, n., -e, pig; das wilde Schwein, boar.

Schweinehirt, m., -en, swineherd.

schwer, heavy.

Schwester, f., -n, sister.

Schwert, n., -er, sword.

schwingen (schwang, geschwungen), to swing.

sechst, sixth.

sechsundzwanzigst, twenty-sixth.

sechzehnt, sixteenth.

See, f., -en, sea, ocean.

Seele, f., -n, soul.

Segringen, name of a village.

sehen (sah, gesehen), to see; sehen auf, to look to, attend to.

Sehnsucht, f., longing.

sehnsüchtig, longing.

sehr, very.

sein* (war, gewesen), to be.

sein, his. its (her).

seiner (gen. of er), of him.

seit (dat.), since, for.

Seite, f., -n, side.

Seitenhieb, m., -e, side cut.

Sekunde, f., -n, second.

selber, self.

selbst, self, even; von —, of its own accord.

seltsam, peculiar.

setzen, to set, put; refl., to sit down.

seufzen, to sigh.

sich, himself, herself, itself, themselves, oneself.

Sicherheit, f., -en, safety.

sie, she, they, them.

sieben, seven.

siebenjährig, seven year (old).

Siegfried, Christian name.

Siegmund, Christian name.

sieh(e)! lo! behold! see sehen.

sieht aus, see aussehen.

sind, see sein.

singen (sang, gesungen), to sing.

sittsam, modest.

sitzen (saß, gesessen), to sit.

Sixtus, proper name.

so, so, then, thus, as; so ... so doch, however ... yet; so so, la la, meaningless expression, so-

so la la; — ein, such a; — ...
wie, just as.

sobald', as soon as.

sogar', even.

sogleich', at once.

Sohn, m., "e, son.

solch, such.

Soldat', m., –en, soldier.

sollen, shall, is to.

Sommer, m., —, summer.

sonderbar, peculiar.

sondern, but.

Sonne, f., –n, sun.

Sonnenuntergang, m., "e, sunset.

Sonntag, m., –e, Sunday.

sonst, else, otherwise, usually, formerly.

Sorge, f., –n, care.

Spaudau, n., proper name.

spann, see spinnen.

Sparsamkeit, f., economy.

spät, late.

später, later on.

Speise, f., –n, food.

Spiel, n., –e, music; play, game.

spielen, to play.

Spieß, m., –e, spit.

Spindel, f., –n, spindle.

spinnen (spann, gesponnen), to spin.

sprach, see sprechen.

Sprachmeister, m., —, language teacher.

sprang, see springen; — herbei, see herbeispringen.

sprechen (sprach, gesprochen), to speak.

springen* (sprang, gesprungen), to jump, run.

Spruch, m., "e, saying, prophecy, wish.

Sprung, m., "e, leap, jump.

stach, see stechen.

Stadt, f., "e, city, town.

stählen, to temper (convert into steel).

Stallung, f., –en, stable.

Stand, m., "e, position, state; imstande sein, to be able.

standen, see stehen.

Star, m., –e, starling.

starb, starben, see sterben.

stark, strong, great.

stärken, to strengthen.

statt (gen.), instead of.

statten; von — gehen, to succeed.

statt-finden (fand, gefunden), to take place.

Staub, m., dust.

stechen (stach, gestochen), refl., to prick oneself.

stecken, to stick, put.

stehen (stand, gestanden), to stand; es stand ihm, it suited him; stehen bleiben, to stop.

steigen* (stieg, gestiegen), to rise, mount.

Stein, m., –e, stone.

Stelle, f., –n, spot, position.

sterben* (starb, gestorben), to die.

Sterbeschachtel, f., –n, coffin.

Stern, m., –e, star.

Stich, m., –e, prick.

stieg, see steigen.

stieß, see stoßen.
still, still, quiet.
stillen, to satisfy.
Stimme, f., –n, voice.
stocken, to stop.
stören, to disturb.
stoßen (stieß, gestoßen), to strike.
Strafanstalt, f., –en, penitentiary, jail.
Strafe, f., –n, punishment
Strand, m., –e, shore.
Strauß, m., ᵉe, bouquet.
streicheln, to stroke.
streng(e), severe.
Strich, m., –e, line, mark.
Strick, m., –e, rope.
striegeln, to groom, comb.
Stroh, n., straw.
Strom, m., ᵉe, stream.
strömen, to flow.
Stübchen, n., —, little room.
Stube, f., –n, room.
Stück, n., –e, piece.
studie'ren, to study.
Stunde, f., –n, hour.
Sturm, m., ᵉe, storm.
stürzen, to rush.
suchen, to seek, look for, try.
Summe, f., –n, sum.

T

Tafel, f., –n, board.
Tag, m., –e, day.
täglich, daily.
tanzen, to dance.
Tänzer, m., —, dancer.
Tänzerin, f., –nen, dancer.
tapfer, brave, courageous.
Tasche, f., –n, pocket.
Tatze, f., –n, paw.
Taube, f., –n, pigeon, dove.
tausend, thousand.
Teich, m., –e, pond.
Teil, m., –e, part.
Teller, m., —, plate.
Thaler, m., —, German dollar.
that, see thun.
Thron, m., –e, throne.
Thorheit, f., –en, folly.
thöricht, foolish.
thun (that, gethan), to do, make.
Thüringen, Thuringia.
Thurm, m., ᵉe, tower.
tief, deep.
Tiefe, f., –en, depth, abyss.
Tier, n., –e, animal.
Tierchen, n., —, dim. of Tier.
Tisch, m., –e, table.
titulie'ren, to call.
Tod, m., death.
tot, dead.
töten, to kill.
Trachten, n., aspiration, aim.
traf, see treffen.
träge, lazy, thick.
tragen (trug, getragen), to carry, wear.
trägt, see tragen.
trank, tranken, see trinken.
trat, see treten.
trat — ein, see eintreten.
traurig, sad.
treffen (traf, getroffen), to hit, meet.

trefflich, excellent.

treiben* (trieb, getrieben), to drift, drive.

trennen, to separate.

treten* (trat, getreten), to step.

trinken (trank, getrunken), to drink; das Trinken, drink, drinking.

Tröpfchen, n., —, little drop; dim. of der Tropfen.

trotz (prep. with gen.), in spite of.

trug — umher, see umhertragen.

tüchtig, good, big.

Tugend, f., –en, virtue.

u

übel, n., —, mischief, misfortune.

über (dat. or acc.), over, at, above, after.

überlaut, excessively loud.

übernehʼmen (übernahm, übernommen), to undertake, assume.

übernomʼmen, see übernehmen.

übertraʼgen (übertrug, übertragen) an, to assign, transfer.

übertruʼgen, see übertragen.

überwieʼgen (überwog, überwogen), to outweigh.

überwogʼ, see überwiegen.

überzieʼhen (überzog, überzogen), to cover.

überzoʼgen, see überziehen.

übrig, over, left.

übrig geblieben, remaining.

um (acc.), about, around; adv., over, past; um — zu, in order to.

umgeben (umgab, umgeben), to surround.

umherʼ-laufen* (lief, gelaufen), to run about.

umherʼ-sehen (sah, gesehen), to look about.

umherʼ-sprangen,* see umher-springen.

umherʼ-springen* (sprang, gesprungen), to jump, play about.

umherʼ-tragen (trug, getragen), to carry around.

um-kehren, refl., to turn around.

um-nieten, to rivet, clinch.

Umstand, m., ⁺e, circumstance.

umziehen (umzog, umzogen), to unbändig, unruly.   [surround.

unbeschädigt, unharmed.

und, and.

undurchdringʼlich, impenetrable.

unendʼlich, infinite, great.

unerbittʼlich, inexorable, pitiless.

unverhofft, unexpected.

ungefähr, about, nearly.

ungerechterweiʼse, unjustly.

Ungetüm, n., –e, monster.

Unglück, n., misfortune.

unglücklicherweiʼse, unfortunately.

Unglücksfall, m., ⁺e, misfortune.

unhöflich, impolite.

unmögʼlich, impossible.

Unruhe, f., restlessness.

unschuldig, innocent.

unser, our.

unten, below.

unter (dat. or acc.), under, by, among.

unterdeſſen, meanwhile.
Unterricht, m., instruction.
unterſtütʒ'en, to support, help.
unterſu'chen, to examine.
unterwegs', on the way.
Unthier, n., –e, monster.
unverſehrt, unharmed.
uralt, very old.

v

Vater, m., ⸗, father.
verachten, to despise.
veraltet, obsolete.
veräußern, to sell.
verbarg, see verbergen.
verbergen (verbarg, verborgen), reſl., to hide.
verbieten (verbot, verboten), to forbid.
verboten, see verbieten.
verbrannt, see verbrennen.
Verbrechen, n., crime.
Verbrecher, m., —, criminal, delinquent.
verbreiten, reſl., to spread.
verbrennen (verbrannte, verbrannt), to burn.
verdang, see verdingen.
verdienen, to deserve, earn.
verdingen (verdang, verdungen), reſl., to engage, enter into service.
verdrießen (verdroß, verdroſſen), to annoy.
verdroß, see verdrießen.
vereinigen, to unite.

verfolgen, to persecute.
verfließen* (verfloß, verfloſſen), to pass.
verfloſſen, see verfließen.
Vergebung, f., pardon.
vergehen* (verging, vergingen, vergangen), to pass away, pass.
vergeſſen (vergaß, vergeſſen), to forget.
verging, see vergehen.
vergleichen (verglich, verglichen), to compare.
Vergnügen, n., —, pleasure.
vergnügt, happy.
vergüten, to compensate, indemnify.
Verlangen, n., demand, desire.
verlangen, to demand, desire.
verlangend, longing.
verlaſſen (verließ, verlaſſen), to leave.
verlieren (verlor, verloren), to lose.
verließ, see verlaſſen.
verloren, see verlieren.
Vermögen, n., property, fortune.
Vermuten, n., expectation.
verpflichten, reſl., to bind oneself.
verroſtet, rusty.
verſah, see verſehen.
verſammeln, reſl., to meet, come together.
verſcheiden* (verſchied, verſchieden) an, to die (of).
verſchied, see verſcheiden.
verſchießen (verſchoß, verſchoſſen) to use up.

verschließen (verschloß, verschlossen), to close, lock.
verschlossen, see verschließen.
verschlucken, to swallow.
verschlingen (verschlang, verschlungen), to devour.
verschönern, to beautify.
verschossen, see verschießen.
verschwinden* (verschwand, verschwunden), to disappear.
verschwunden, see verschwinden.
versehen (versah, versehen), *refl.*, to make a mistake, provide; with *gen. obj.*, to be aware of.
versetzen, to reply.
versiegelt, sealed.
verspotten, to mock, make fun of.
versprach, see versprechen.
versprechen (versprach, versprochen), to promise.
Verstand, *m.*, mind, intellect, understanding.
verstand, see verstehen.
verständig, intelligent.
verstehen (verstand, verstanden), to understand; *refl.* (auf), to understand, be good at.
verstopfen, to stop up, obstruct.
versuchen, to try.
Verteidigung, *f.*, defence.
vertragen (vertrug, vertragen), *refl.*, to get along together.
Vertrauen, *n.*, confidence, trust.
verurteilen, to condemn.
verwandeln, to change.
Verwandte, *m.*, –n, relative.

verwunden, to wound.
verwundern, *refl.*, to wonder.
verwundert, astonished.
Verwunderung, *f.*, wonder.
viel, much, many.
vielleicht', perhaps.
vielmehr', rather, much more.
Viertelstunde, *f.*, –n, quarter of an hour.
Vogel, *m.*, ¨, bird.
Vogelsteller, *m.*, —, fowler.
Vöglein, *n.*, —, little bird.
Volk, *n.*, ¨er, people.
voll (*gen.*), full of, full.
vollends, besides.
vollkom'men, perfect, absolute.
von (*dat.*), from, of, by (*passive*).
vor (*dat.* or *acc.*), before, for, with.
vorbei', by, past.
Vorfall, *m.*, ¨e, experience.
vor=haben (hatte, gehabt), to intend, want.
Vorhang, *m.*, ¨e, curtain.
vorig, former, preceding.
vor=kommen* (kam, gekommen), seem, happen.
vor=legen, to lay before one, ask.
vor=lesen (las, gelesen), to read aloud, read to.
vorn, in front.
Vorrat, *m.*, ¨e, store, supply.
Vorsicht, *f.*, caution.
vor=tragen (trug, getragen), to state, tell.

vortreff'lich, excellent, admirable.

vorwärts, forward.

vor-ziehen (zog, gezogen), to prefer, close.

w

Wache, f., -n, watch.

wachen, to watch.

wachsen* (wuchs, gewachsen), to grow.

Waffe, f., -n, arm, weapon.

Waffenschmied, m., -e, armorer.

wagen, to dare.

wahr, true, real.

während, prep. with gen., during; conj., while.

Wald, m., "er, forest.

Wand, f., "e, wall.

Wanderer, m., —, wanderer.

wann? when?

war, see sein.

warb, see werben.

warf, see werfen.

Warnungsquietschen, n., squeak of warning.

warten, to wait.

warum'? why?

was? what?

Wasser, n., water.

Watte, f., cotton.

wedeln (mit), to wag.

weder . . . noch, neither . . . nor.

Weg, m., -e, way.

weg, away.

wegen (gen.), on account of.

weg-laufen* (lief, gelaufen), to run away.

weg-nehmen (nahm, genommen), to take away.

weg-tragen (trug, getragen), to carry off.

Wegweiser, m., —, guide.

wehe-thun (that, gethan), to hurt.

wehren, refl., to defend oneself.

Weib, n., -er, woman, wife.

Weide, f., -n, meadow, pasture.

Weidmesser, n., —, hunting-knife.

weil, because.

Weilchen, n., —, little while.

Weile, f., while.

Wein, m., -e, wine.

weinen, to weep.

Weise, m., -n, wise man.

weise, wise.

Weise, f., -n, manner.

weiß, white.

weit, far, wide, broad

weiter, further, on.

weiter-gehen* (ging, gegangen), to go, pass on.

weiter-kriechen* (kroch, gekrochen), to creep on.

weithin, far (off).

welch, which, who, what.

Welt, f., -en, world.

Weltmeer, n., -e, Ocean.

Wendeltreppe, f., -n, winding staircase.

wenig, little.

wenigstens, at least.

wenn, if, when.

wer, who; rel., he who.

werden* (warb or wurde, geworden), to become; *aux.*, to
be, shall, will.

werfen (warf, geworfen), to throw.

wert, worth.

wessen (*gen.* of wer), whose.

Westen, *m.*, West.

Wetter, *n.*, weather.

Wettrennen, *n.*, —, race.

Wettstreit, *m.*, competition

wetzen, to whet.

wider, against.

wie, how? like, as, how.

wieder, again, back.

wieder-erkennen, (erkannte, erkannt), to recognize.

wieder=finden (fand, gefunden), to
find again.

wiederho'len, to repeat.

wiederum, again.

Wieland, proper name.

wild, wild, savage.

Wildbret, *n.*, game.

Wildnis, *f.*, wilderness.

will, see wollen.

Wille(n), *m.*, will.

willst, see wollen.

wimmeln von, *imp.*, to swarm

Wind, *m.*, -e, wind.   [with.

Winkel, *m.*, —, corner.

winken (*dat.*), to beckon.

winseln, to whine.

Winter, *m.*, —, winter.

wir, we.

wirklich, real.

wissen (wußte, gewußt; *pres.* ich
weiß), to know.

Witwe, *f.*, -n, widow.

Witwenstand, *m.*, widowhood.

wo, where, when.

Woche, *f.*, -n, week.

wogen, to rush.

woher', whence, wherefrom.

wohl, well, easily, probably,
perhaps, I presume.

wohlbehalten, safe, unhurt.

wohlthätig, benevolent, generous.

wohlzufrieden, well satisfied.

wohnen, to live.

Wolf, *m.*, ⁻e, wolf.

Wolke, *f.*, -n, cloud.

Wolle, *f.*, wool.

wollen (*pres.* ich will), to be willing, want, wish.

Wort, *n.*, -e or ⁻er, word.

worüber, of what, about what.

worum', about what, for what.

Wörtlein, *n.*, —, little word.

wovon', of which.

wuchs, see wachsen.

Wunde, *f.*, -n, wound.

Wunder, *n.*, —, wonder.

Wundergabe, *f.*, -n, wonderful
gift.

Wunderkästchen, *n.*, —, magic box.

wunderlich, peculiar,

wundern, *refl.*, to wonder.

wunderschön, very beautiful.

Wunsch, *m.*, ⁻e, wish.

wünschen, to wish.

wurde, wurden, see werden.

Wüste, *f.*, -n, desert.

wüßte, see wissen.

wütend, furious.

3

zahlen, to pay.
zählen, to count.
zahm, tame.
zähmen, to tame.
Zahmheit, f., tameness.
Zahn, m., ⸗e, tooth.
zart, delicate, light.
zärtlich, tender.
Zauberspruch, m., ⸗e, charm, magic spell.
z. B. (zum Beispiel), for example.
zehn, ten.
zeichnen, to mark.
zeigen, to show; — auf, to point to.
Zeit, f., -en, time.
Zelt, n., -e, tent.
Zettel, m., —, slip of paper.
zerbrach, see zerbrechen.
zerbrechen (zerbrach, zerbrochen), to break.
zerbrichst, see zerbrechen.
zerreißen (zerriß, zerrissen), to tear.
zerrissen, see zerreißen.
zerschellen, to shatter.
zersprang, see zerspringen.
zerspringen* (zersprang, zersprungen), to burst.
ziehen (zog, gezogen), to draw, pull; ziehen*, travel, go.
Ziel, n., -e, aim.
zierlich, pretty, dainty.
Zimmer, n., —, room.
zog, see ziehen.

zu (dat.), at, to, for; zu — hinaus, out through; adv., too.
Zufall, m., ⸗e, chance.
zu⸗geben (gab, gegeben), to permit.
zu⸗gehen* (ging, gegangen), to happen, move.
zu⸗gesellen, to join, place with.
zugleich', at the same time.
zu⸗greifen (griff, gegriffen), to help oneself, seize.
zu⸗hauen (hieb, gehauen), to strike.
zuletzt', at last, finally.
zum = zu dem, zu einem.
zumal', especially.
Zumpt, proper name.
zu⸗nicken, to nod to.
zur = zu der.
zurück'⸗bleiben* (blieb, geblieben), to remain behind.
zurück'⸗bringen (brachte, gebracht), to bring back, return.
zurück'⸗geben (gab, gegeben), to give back, return.
zurück'⸗laufen* (lief, gelaufen), to run back.
zurück'⸗ziehen (zog, gezogen), to draw back.
zusam'men, together.
zusam'men⸗ducken, refl., to crouch down.
zusam'men⸗halten (hielt, gehalten), to hold together.
zusam'men⸗lesen (las, gelesen), to gather.
zusam'men⸗raffen, to collect.
zusam'men⸗thun (that, gethan), to close.

zu-ſehen (ſah, geſehen), to look at, watch.

zu-ſpitzen, to point.

Zuſpruch, *m.*, ⁻e, custom.

zu-tragen (trug, getragen), *refl.*, *imp.*, to happen.

zuvor', first before.

zuvor'kommend, thoughtful, obliging.

zuwei'len, sometimes.

zwar, indeed, of course, to be sure, however, that is.

zwei, two.

Zweig, *m.*, –e, branch.

zweit, second.

zwiſchen (*dat.* or *acc.*), between.

zwölf, twelve.

zwölft, twelfth.

GRAMMATICAL APPENDIX.

---

1. In simple German words the accent usually rests on the radical syllable.

2. In compound German words (except adverbs) the accent usually rests on the radical syllable of the first component.

Declension of Nouns.

3. *Genitive singular:*

(*a*) Masculine nouns that take ⸗(e)n to form the plural take this ending also in the genitive, dative and accusative singular.

(*b*) Feminine nouns have the same form in all cases of the singular.

(*c*) Masculine and neuter nouns usually form the genitive singular by adding ⸗ß or ⸗eß. Though most of these nouns may take either ending the following rules must be observed:

> The ending ⸗eß is preferred in monosyllabic nouns, but it *must* be added to nouns ending in a hissing sound: baß Glaß, *gen.* beß Glaſeß.
>
> The ending ⸗ß (never ⸗eß) *must* be added to nouns

107

ending in a syllable with unaccented ⸗e (⸗er, ⸗el, ⸗en, ⸗enb, ⸗em, ⸗chen, also ⸗lein); thus, daß Mädchen, *gen.* deß Mädchens, never Mädchenes.

4. *Dative singular:*

Masculine and neuter nouns (except those referred to in § 8a) may take the ending ⸗e in the dative singular. Though this ending may be omitted at pleasure, it must never be added to nouns ending in a syllable with un-accented ⸗e ⸗(er, ⸗el, ⸗en, ⸗enb, ⸗em, ⸗chen, ⸗lein); thus, bem Bater, never bem Batere.

5. *Accusative singular:*

The accusative singular is always like the nominative except with masculine nouns adding ⸗en to form the plural.

6. *Plural:*

Masculines:	⸗er, ⸗el, ⸗en	—
	⸗e, and a few monosyllables	–(e)n
	foreign words with final accent	–en
	about a dozen monosyllables	^{x}er
	All others (with few exceptions)	^{x}e
Feminines:	Mutter and Tochter	^{x}
	about 30 monosyllables	^{x}e
	All others	–en
Neuters:	⸗er, ⸗el, ⸗en, ⸗chen, ⸗lein	—
	about 50 nouns, mostly monosyllables . . .	^{x}er
	All others (with few exceptions)	–e

7. The dative plural takes the ending ⸗n, unless the noun already ends in n.

DECLENSION OF ADJECTIVES.

8. The *limiting* adjectives have only one declension, commonly called the *strong* declension of adjectives:

	Singular			Plural
	m.	*f.*	*n.*	*m. f. n.*
Nom.	–er	–e	–es	–e
Gen.	–es	–er	–es	–er
Dat.	–em	–er	–em	–en
Acc.	–en	–e	–es	–e

9. There is a slight difference in some of the endings of the definite article:

	Singular			Plural
	m.	*f.*	*n.*	*m. f. n.*
Nom.	der	die	das	die
Gen.	des	der	des	der
Dat.	dem	der	dem	den
Acc.	den	die	das	die

10. The indefinite article, all possessive adjectives, and fein, also differ, having no endings in the singular of the nominative masculine and the nominative and accusative neuter:

	Singular			Plural
	m.	*f.*	*n.*	*m. f. n.*
Nom.	ein	eine	ein	feine
Gen.	eines	einer	eines	feiner
Dat.	einem	einer	einem	feinen
Acc.	einen	eine	ein	feine

11. All *qualifying* adjectives have two declensions, the strong and the weak. They have the strong declension, i.e. the declension of the limiting adjectives, when they stand alone before the noun, or when the preceding limiting adjective is without endings; in all other cases they have the weak declension:

	Singular			*Plural*
	m.	*f.*	*n.*	*m. f. n.*
Nom.	–e	–e	–e	–en
Gen.	–en	–en	–en	–en
Dat.	–en	–en	–en	–en
Acc.	–en	–e	–n	–en

12. Paradigms of declension:

Singular

Nom.	der kluge Fuchs	die kleine Ameise	das edle Pferd
Gen.	des klugen Fuchses	der kleinen Ameise	des edlen Pferdes
Dat.	dem klugen Fuchse	der kleinen Ameise	dem edlen Pferd
Acc.	den klugen Fuchs	die kleine Ameise	das edle Pferd

Plural

Nom.	die klugen Füchse	die kleinen Ameisen	die edlen Pferde
Gen.	der klugen Füchse	der kleinen Ameisen	der edlen Pferde
Dat.	den klugen Füchsen	den kleinen Ameisen	den edlen Pferden
Acc.	die klugen Füchse	die kleinen Ameisen	die edlen Pferde

Singular

Nom.	ein sterbender Löwe	eine kleine Maus	ein schönes Haus
Gen.	eines sterbenden Löwen	einer kleinen Maus	eines schönen Hauses
Dat.	einem sterbenden Löwen	einer kleinen Maus	einem schönen Haus
Acc.	einen sterbenden Löwen	eine kleine Maus	ein schönes Haus

Plural

Nom.	sterbende Löwen	kleine Mäuse	schöne Häuser
Gen.	sterbender Löwen ·	kleiner Mäuse	schöner Häuser
Dat.	sterbenden Löwen	kleinen Mäusen	schönen Häusern
Acc.	sterbende Löwen	kleine Mäuse	schöne Häuser

GERMAN.

Freytag's Die Journalisten.

Lustspiel in vier Akten.　With Introduction, Notes, and Vocabulary.　By T. B. BRONSON, A.M., Head of Modern Language Department, Lawrenceville (N. J.) School. 16mo.　Cloth, 45 cents

The student requires only such helps as are essential for comprehending the text; not a redundance of annotations, but sufficient to sharpen his thought and give him a broad grasp of the grammar and syntax of the language, as well as of its idiomatic use.　It is with such purpose that this edition of Freytag's "Die Journalisten" was prepared.　Other distinctive features are the clear and handsome typography, the comprehensive introduction to Freytag's life and writings, the outline of the argument preceding each act, foot-notes on all points needing elucidation, and a complete vocabulary, with the principal parts of the irregular verbs, and the pronunciation of the words where there may be any uncertainty.

Goethe's Hermann und Dorothea.

By ARTHUR H. PALMER, M.A., Yale University.　16mo.　Cloth, 50 cents.

The animating purpose in preparing this edition of one of Goethe's best poems was to make its reading easy and enjoyable for its own sake.　The Introduction and Notes are concise, but practical and helpful, while to the Vocabulary has been given the most careful attention in order to make it complete, accurate, and thoroughly satisfactory.

D. APPLETON AND COMPANY,

NEW YORK.　　BOSTON.　　CHICAGO.　　LONDON.

GERMAN.

Lessing's Minna von Barnhelm.

With Introduction, Notes, and Vocabulary. By CHARLES BUNDY WILSON, A.M., Professor of German Language and Literature in the State University of Iowa. Illustrated. 16mo. Cloth, 50 cents.

"Minna von Barnhelm" is recognized as the best German comedy, and as it was also the first national comedy it occupies a very important place in the history of German literature. In preparing this edition an effort has been made to lead the student to an appreciation of Lessing's drama as a masterpiece of literary art. The introduction discusses, among other things, the historical background, the literary significance of "Minna von Barnhelm," the sources of the plot, the characters, the language, and the criticisms of contemporary and recent writers. The notes, which have been placed at the bottom of the page to avoid the necessity of a double reference to the back part of the book, draw attention to peculiarities of idiom, and explain all ordinary difficulties. The appended vocabulary is complete, and the illustrations have been selected with care.

Schiller's Die Jungfrau von Orleans.

Eine Romantische Tragödie. With Introduction, Notes, and Vocabulary. By LEWIS A. RHOADES, Ph.D., Professor of German in the University of Illinois. Illustrated. 16mo Cloth, 60 cents.

"Die Jungfrau von Orleans" is one of the most interesting and poetic dramas in the German language. Its subject-matter, as well as its literary form, appeals strongly to the pupil, and makes it an especially suitable introduction to the works of Schiller. This edition has been adapted to the needs of high schools, and, in the introduction, material has been supplied to explain the historical setting of the drama and its merit as a masterpiece of literary art.

D. APPLETON AND COMPANY,

NEW YORK.   BOSTON.   CHICAGO.   LONDON.